Somewhere South of Tuscany

Five Years in a Four-Cat Town

Diana G. Armstrong

In order to protect the privacy of the inhabitants of Lubriano, certain characters and places have fictitious names and identifying characteristics.

Library of Congress Number: 2010902317

ISBN: 1439266212

First Edition
Published in the United States of America

To my husband David

Also by Diana G. Armstrong:

Cooking for My Friends – Casual Healthy Entertaining
(1998)
ISBN 0-9664650-0-8

FOREWORD

In the 1960s, I received a most unusual package in the mail. It was a collection of letters written by my grandmother Mary Blackwood Dick in the 1880s. Through a strange and merciful set of circumstances, these letters survived. She had written them as she traveled into the heart of Africa to marry her fiancé, my grandfather, who at that time was fighting in Rhodesia (now Zimbabwe) for Cecil Rhodes against the local Matabele and Mashona tribes.

She was *simpatico* with all the local people and their ways, and accepting of her new surroundings. This has resonated deeply with me, through my youth in South Africa, my middle years living in the USA, and my "new" life in a small village in Italy. Given my unintentional nomadic life, she indeed taught me an extremely useful lesson: there is no single way to do a thing. The right way is the way it is done in the place you are in at that moment.

Over these many years, I have drawn much comfort and enjoyment from these letters. So I felt the need to record too, a small but unusual part of my life, comfortable in the knowledge that somewhere down the road, *my* grandchildren may pick up this book and be tempted by an old recipe, but more importantly, have a good laugh.

Diana G. Armstrong
Lubriano, Italy 2010

Somewhere South of Tuscany
Five Years in a Four-Cat Town

Contents

Don't you see, Signora?
In the village, we know...
These things, they are us, and they are all the same:

Campagna (the countryside)

Compagno (a companion)

Con Pane (with bread)

1

SONO QUI – I AM HERE

The fog slides away by midmorning. The square is in shade except for shallow sunshine pasted on the front of the Church. Two old men, hands in pockets, are flattened against the wall. I walk past them down the road to Via Roma 17, down the cobbled street, my two suitcases bouncing behind me. I cut off the top of a letter with our names printed on it and tape it onto the buzzer.

2

MAX

I have been putting up with Max for five years now—these five years since I taped my name onto the buzzer of Via Roma 17.

There he is, again, in his too-tight pants, sunglasses on top of his head, knowing I will find him.

Max nags as he drives me away, hands flying off the wheel in the Italian way that is mandatory while talking. What's more, I would prefer it if he, while talking, did not look me directly in the eye as I sit in the seat behind him.

"What about this terrible traffic around Fiumicino?" he says.

"These Italians are crazy mad drivers!" he says (even though he is Italian himself).

"It is really inconvenient that the American flights arrive at around eight in the morning."

And so he goes, on and on—that he has to deal with all this *disastro* and is really in need of a good espresso, especially the one that he did not have time to get this morning, which was made by his mother. We stop at a gas station so that he can purchase one. He pulls a face as he swigs it back, as though he has just gulped a cup of lemon juice by mistake.

Complaint follows complaint as he flies through congested streets and exits the *Autostrada* at Orvieto. Gas prices are too high. His brother is a jerk. His mother is depressed. The government is crazy. He has no time to find a girlfriend.

He drops me one more time at Via Roma 17 Lubriano. In his hurry to get back to Rome, he flings my suitcases just inside the front door.

It is a relief to see his van take off, leaving a tire burn down the narrow cobbled street.

I take a deep breath and feel my stress leave with him in the form of imaginary tin cans attached to his bumper.

Our life in an Italian village definitely bears reflection.

3

CAVEAT EMPTOR

Let the buyer beware!   *(Roman proverb)*

I have arranged to meet Signor Galli, our realtor, for a final walkthrough before closing. He is trying not to look astonished. Why would I want to see the house again? I have seen it once already. But I stand my ground. I don't entirely trust the seller, Signora Morelli.

My son Richard is with me. He is in a transitional stage best described as a "writer/backpacker leaning towards computer programming" phase. He is in no hurry to find himself, for he knows he ultimately will. He is a big, comfortable presence, very relaxed as he quietly rambles on about the difference between super-assertive Umbrian and softer, more fragrant Tuscan olive oils.

We leave our hotel in Orvieto and take the drive to Lubriano, just south of Tuscany and just east of Umbria. We drive just ten minutes into Tuscia, the ancient Etruscan homeland. We wind through dormant vineyards and olive groves silver in the cold February light.

I meet Signor Galli, who is, as my Italian friend puts it, "cutting a dashing figure." There he stands, leaning on what will hopefully soon be our old iron gate set in an old *basaltina* black stone archway. The IHS crest of the Jesuits carved into the stone at the top of the arch completes in my mind an advertisement for some Italian men's cologne. This old Jesuit building, Signor Galli thinks, was built in around 1600 as a monastery.

"But how old?" I ask.

"This building, it is very old!" he says, and I leave it at that.

We enter through the iron gate. We climb the *basaltina* stairs to the front door. The stone steps are worn low and smooth by many feet. The stairs are topped by a small black and white kitten sitting proprietarily. We enter into a courtyard—a gathering place for monks in centuries past, I am sure. The thick *tufa* walls are a patch-up job of old stone doorways sealed up, and others opened for reasons that must have been important to someone at the time. Our home is to the right, and to the left are our neighbors-to-be.

Signor Galli opens the front door, impatiently fumbling with some very large, old rusty keys which he had hidden from view, so as, I think, not to destroy his image.

My suspicions about Signora Morelli are soon justified. Despite my signed offer stating that "nothing in the house is to be removed or even unscrewed," she has pretty well stripped the place bare. Instead of "unscrewing" the old iron curtain rods, she has ripped them out, leaving big holes in the walls. (Well, at least she didn't *unscrew* them.) She has also removed all the mirrors and the light bulbs.

One item remains in the kitchen—an old ceramic sink suspended in midair, with an unrelated faucet sticking out of the wall. An old chestnut roaster has been thrown into the fireplace. As I reach in to examine it, I look up the chimney and see daylight and the possibility that a large Santa and much cold air could easily make their ways down.

Signor Galli is agitated; one shoulder is jiggling so that his linen jacket almost slips off its perch on the edge of his shoulders.

At least my eleventh-hour viewing has satisfied me that I distrust Signora Morelli. I know now more clearly what I had not seen when I viewed it for the first time: Signor Galli is right. This place is very old. This place, I find out later, is as old as St. Peter's Basilica in Rome.

There are French doors, all with sweeping views out across a valley. The hilltop town of Civita di Bagnoregio is jutting out of the mist like a sandcastle ready to be washed away.

There is a fresco on the living room ceiling. A life-sized winged angel with a shield and a sword and a most serene look on her face is gazing gently down on me. Her sweet face makes her look more like a kindly saint than the Goddess of War. The colors are warm, earthy maroons and deep, old greens. The fresco provides sad evidence that many Italians don't appreciate what is old and precious; someone has chipped a channel into the fresco to wire a light fixture right in the middle of the goddess's bellybutton.

As we leave, I spot our neighbors-to-be in the little courtyard we will share with them. They are attending to their potted plants, which fill the courtyard with color and greenery. I think they are there to sneak a look at us, these mysterious strangers who have unaccountably arrived in their village and in their courtyard.

With looks of surprise, they come over to greet us. Signor Galli is in attendance. The Signora, about seventy, is vivacious, very slim, and wearing jeans and silver nail polish, and the Signore is also slim, in slippers, quiet, and a little bent-over. They have a cotton cloth carefully laid on top of their doormat to prevent it from getting dirty.

They give us a great welcome in rapid-fire Italian and launch into an enthusiastic but completely incomprehensible conversation. They're very happy to have new neighbors. Signora Morelli, the seller of our home, has not been in residence for a long time, and appears to have had no interest in any upkeep or maintenance of the property. It's also clear from their change in demeanor at the mention of her name that she has been a difficult neighbor. There have been problems, for sure. What they are or were we cannot guess, and at this late stage, quite frankly, I don't want to know.

Signor Galli keeps on looking at his shoes, shuffling a little as we chat with them. They are the Gasparis. We suspect that Signora Gaspari may have given this preamble to other prospective buyers. Signor Galli seems unwilling to translate, and whole sentences spouted by them are transformed by him into one word. Each comment by Signora Gaspari is accompanied by much hand clasping and hand wagging.

With lots of "*Saluti*" we escape to our tumbled-down garden-to-be behind our house. It is scattered with furry, pitted stones and an alarming number of tree stumps. A low, moss-covered wall at the far end of the property overlooks a gentle field and perilously holds the property from falling into a valley below. There is a stream trickling somewhere down there, and a huge fig tree reaches over the wall and into the garden, kindly offering its shade and hopefully its fruit to us.

It's clear that the garden, as they say, needs work. Signora Morelli's junk is scattered all over the place. Old, broken, rusty tables and chairs are props for weeds. We have been warned that when a property changes hands in Italy, the seller will leave anything and everything he doesn't want to bother to take, and it is up to the buyer to sort it all out and get rid of it. This is the good news and the bad news; the good news is that there are endless stacks, perhaps with some old treasure hidden in them, and the bad news is that there are endless stacks.

Now I look over the empty home. It has been four months since we signed an Italian version of an offer, called a *compromesso*, which in Signora Morelli's case is anything but a compromise. She has interpreted the document with flair and creativity.

4

FROM *ATTO* TO *CONTRATTO*

Our appointment is in the late afternoon in nearby Viterbo, a walled city famous for its medieval Palace of the Popes. We are here for the closing. All the traffic is stopped as a motorcade passes before us—the retinue of the Italian Prime Minister. He too has chosen this day to visit Viterbo, and all we can do is wait impatiently as the line of big, black cars threads slowly through the narrow streets. The procession passes, and the local police, the *Carabinieri*, step into the street and wave us on. They all look like major-generals in the armed forces.

In spite of this delay, we arrive an hour early for our appointment. We find the office of the

Notaio—the Notary—locked and dark. It is the quiet and civilized time during which nothing much happens in Italy. A neighborhood bar fortifies us with a glass of wine. We explain to the owner that we are waiting to sign an *atto*, a bill of sale for our new house. With a flourish, he produces a bottle of *spumante* - sparkling wine and shows it to us. It's called *Contratto*—Contract. We like that name, *Contratto*. We hope it's a good omen. Not wanting to be jinxed, we ask him to save it for later.

We return to the *Notaio's* office for our five o'clock appointment. I check my documents again: passport, checkbook, Italian ID card, even a copy of my Italian bank statement, plus a stack of other papers. We are quite a contingent, six of us in all. Our friend Peter Dixon, an English lawyer who lives in Italy, is with us. He is frightfully well-spoken, with bright blue eagle eyes and matching beak, a reassuring presence. Apart from him there is our son Richard, Signor Galli and his assistant with her patchy English, and my Italian lawyer, Dr. Ricci. I feel as though I have enough people with me to buy a small country.

At five o'clock on the dot, the door opens again and the *Notaio* makes his entrance. He is a large, impressive man who looks very much like Samuel Johnson and has the same booming voice for which Johnson was famous. He would look great with an English lawyer's wig on. His offices are quite imposing, with heavy paneling and glass cases filled with books. There are four elegant and worn red leather sofas. The office imparts unease in the face of the law, but we have a greater cause for misgiving. Where is Signora Morelli?

Although I have never met her, I know she is over 80, and I picture her as about five feet tall, a little overweight, clad in black, and possibly having taken off her shawl for this special occasion. Perhaps she is having difficulty making it up the stairs.

There is a long, painful silence. Then the door opens again, and Signora Morelli sweeps into the room. I stare at her in awe. Tall, elegant, and well-dressed, she looks at least twenty years younger than she is. In spite of myself, I feel a little intimidated. Her son, middle-aged and diffident, creeps in behind her. He looks intimidated, too.

Notaio Allessandro ushers us into his office, a little startled at the large contingent of people. We arrange ourselves around the desk and the reading of the *atto* begins. It's conducted in Italian, and it goes on and on at great length. Every so often, Signora Morelli breaks in, wearing a contemptuous look, and my lawyer jumps in to deal with her objections. I'm extremely happy to have an Italian lawyer on one side of me and my Italian-speaking friend Peter on the other. I can see that Peter is ready to snatch at any hint of impropriety on anybody's part.

Signora Morelli is visibly angered by something in the proceedings. Perhaps she is bothered that she is selling to foreigners. She is unabashedly sizing me up, skepticism all over her face. Then it comes out in a torrent of Italian. She will not agree to sell the house to us unless we also buy her cantina as part of the deal!

I'm baffled. I explain to my lawyer that we had originally tried to get the cantina included in the deal, but Signora Morelli had peremptorily refused to even discuss it. Confusion reigns in the office—everyone is talking at once. The lawyer and notary try to explain to Signora Morelli that the documents before us cannot be altered at this point. She refuses to listen. Even her son tries to reason with her. She silences him with a glare.

Finally my lawyer rises to his feet. Either Signora Morelli signs the documents as agreed, or we are leaving. The room falls silent, and I hold my breath. Grudgingly, Signora Morelli mutters her assent, and the crisis passes. The closing continues. Time drags on; each word is read aloud and then translated for my benefit, until at last the end of the document is reached. At a sign from the lawyer, I produce the check from my purse, and hand it to the notary. Signora Morelli promptly voices another objection. After more confusion, it emerges that she won't accept the check. She refuses to believe that I have enough money in the bank to cover it. Although she has no right to ask for it, I hold out my bank statement, secretly congratulating myself on my foresight in having thought to bring it with me. She takes the document and looks suspiciously at the foot of the page.

Suddenly her son leaps to his feet and snatches it out of her hand. His meekness forgotten, he berates her furiously. Even without knowing any Italian, it's clear that, simply by looking at the proffered document, she has crossed some line of honorable behavior and embarrassed the family.

The son turns to me, bows imperceptibly, and hands back the document with studied courtesy, making sure that we all see that *he*, at least, has not looked at it. Mercifully, this incident seems to deflate Signora Morelli, and the rest of the ceremony proceeds without further problems. I hand over the check, which she accepts with some ill grace; documents are passed around for signatures and returned to the notary. He pulls out a tray of large rubber stamps, inks them liberally, stamps all the documents loudly, and signs them with a flourish.

These formalities, performed with an air of great importance, seem to preclude any further discussion, negotiation, or objection. With immense gravity, the notary hands me a large iron key. That's all. No receipt for my check, no documents, no copy of the agreement—just a big, rusty key, although an impressive one to be sure, about six inches long and heavy in my hand. Some blacksmith must have fashioned it many years ago, and it feels almost like a piece of history as I walk out of the office clutching it tightly.

After two hours of Morelli aggravation, *Notaio* reading, and *atto* signing, we walk out happy and head straight across the narrow old street, right into the bar. It feels good to have Signora Morelli's antics behind us once and for all (or at least so we think at the time!). We have made it all the way from *atto* to *contratto*.

❧❧

I call my husband David back in the USA to tell him we own a house that he has never seen. During his career, we have been the victims of a corporate relocation program that has moved us nine times in twenty-five years. David has long since given up his right to preview houses. That is trust. It takes two to navigate through life, and it's good to be able to depend on the person with the other oar. Successful journeys build trust. And so it is with David and me.

The owner of *il Bar* is standing in his doorway when we arrive. I show him the key, and he breaks into a broad grin.

"*Auguri, auguri!*" he says—Congratulations!

The bottle of *Contratto spumante* is produced from the fridge, and we all drink a toast, or a *brindisi*, as I soon learn to call it. We finish the wine and try to pay for it. Just come back and visit him another time, he says. And so we leave.

With some trepidation, secretly wondering if it will fit, I put the big six-inch key into the door and turn it. The old wooden door swings wide open.

5

THE REST IS HISTORY

"Lubriano," says my local guidebook dismissively, "is not mentioned in the historic record until the year 1025."

Well! This may make it a newcomer kind of place around these parts, but by our standards this is pretty impressive.

We read on. The author admits, somewhat grudgingly, that archeology has shown that the oldest settlements in the town date from the Etruscans—from oh, say, about 500 BC. The history of the area for the next twenty-five centuries makes one cringe. The town is too close to Rome for its own safety. This part of the Etruscan state was conquered by Rome in 265

BC, then conquered again by most of the nasty people we remember from our history books. The Goths, the Vandals, the Visigoths, the Longobardi, and lots of other unwelcome invaders came through here, visiting destruction on the poor Lubrianese. Finally Charlemagne imposed order on the area, and the Benedictines took over in 824. We find that this ancient history comes much more startlingly to life when we are standing upon the very ground where it took place.

From ancient times the little towns of the Calanchi have been perched precariously on their hilltops along this ancient and violent border, in danger of toppling backward into the lap of Rome or forward into Umbria. But this is an illusion. When Rome was nothing but a modest settlement at a convenient crossing point on the Tiber, the towns of the Calanchi were well established. Their founders, the Etruscans, had carefully chosen these apparently inhospitable hilltops and cliff edges to build their towns. One of these towns is Lubriano, a modest settlement even by the standards of the Calanchi. At its height, the town boasted two thousand people, and today there are eight hundred souls. Looking at the town from across the valley, you can see Lubriano's cliffs, honeycombed with looted Etruscan tombs. Apart from the lootings, nothing much has changed here. The town has survived admirably perched on its narrow ridge of *tufa* rock—the same golden rock from which every medieval building in Umbria is built. The ridge of the Lubriano hamlet is small, half a mile end-to-end and only a couple of hundred feet wide. To the south, facing Rome, the town is protected by the cliffs, and to the north, with Orvieto in the distance, the town is protected by the gentle green Umbrian river valley.

The valley lies only a hundred miles or so from Rome, and marks the border between the flat plains of the Tiber Valley and the folded hills of Umbria. Here we are in ancient Latium, sandwiched between Umbria and Tuscany, only a hundred miles from Rome but seemingly ten times that in sensibility.

6

FINDING LUBRIANO

Over a decade ago we found ourselves in the hilltop town of Orvieto. This day proves to present one of life's crossroads. Orvieto is one of the stately cities of Italy, medieval, cobbled, with a welcoming ambience, a spectacular setting, and a history stretching back in time. It is filled with impressive buildings from every era, but is dominated in every respect by its massive Romanesque *duomo*—cathedral. Its mosaic-encrusted edifice was built to house a humble altar cloth, the relic of a long-ago miracle, which is tucked away in one of its chapels.

Down a narrow side street we pause to look at a realtor's advertisement. "*Casa Affita*" says a small sign in a shadow box between two ceramics emporiums. There are several faded photos of houses. Some are for rent, some are for sale; some seem to be in good condition, others less so. Some appear to resemble piles of rubble, but are optimistically described as "partially restored." Given a choice between a pushy realtor and a bunch of ceramics vendors, my husband David goes for the realtor. I go for the ceramics. He slips up the dark staircase and follows the realtor's billboards to a landing.

To his amazement, the office above is a cool haven from the over-decorated street below. Out steps a rather attractive girl, who invites him in. The day is looking up. She introduces him to the realtor, Signor Galli, who is sitting like a Hollywood casting director at a desk made entirely of glass. The walls and floor of the office are simple terracotta. There is not a Tuscan curl to be seen in the place. He has crystal-blue eyes and a calm presence. He offers David a glass of cool wine and an impressive leather-bound album filled with photos, mainly duplicate photos of the piles of rubble in the shadow box below.

David flips through the photos, passing the time. One photo gets his attention. It is a picture of a charming two-hundred-year-old farmhouse, available for rent. It was a working farm, Signor Galli says, and now the house is restored. Where the cattle were housed there is a living room, he adds, which makes it sound a little suspicious. It is called a *casale*—country house, he says. It is not a villa.

Chapter 6

Signor Galli offers to take David to view the property. It is only fifteen minutes away from Orvieto, out in the fields and vineyards. The price, quoted in lire, appears outrageous, but after a conversion to dollars, David sees that the weekly rent is actually very reasonable. We've heard that in parts of neighboring Tuscany, the British are renting villas in such vast numbers that the Chianti region sometimes is sarcastically referred as "Chiantishire."

We are excited at the thought of a vacation in this beautiful old house, and we decide to rent it in the fall, three months later. We are in the middle of making plans for this trip when David has one of his all-too-frequent work-related crises and can't get away to Italy. Hastily we revise our plans; since we have already paid for the farmhouse, I invite five girlfriends to accompany me there. I try to moderate their expectations. My mantra is "This is *not* a villa!" I hand them a test to see if they are up for an Italian countryside experience. It is the owner's note warning us "please to be patient" because "this is the country and some mouses may get in the house."

We fly to Rome and take the train to Orvieto. Signor Galli is waiting next to his shiny Land Rover to pick us up from the train station in Orvieto and escort us to the house. In his well-cut suit and blue silk tie, he looks dashing.

"*Come sta?*" he says, with a simultaneous vestigial heel click.

He opens the door of the Land Rover with an elegant gesture, and two of my friends quickly jump in.

I suspect that getting ladies to jump into his car is seldom difficult for the gallant Signor Galli. Those of us who moved too slowly pile into the shoebox-sized rental car and follow with the suitcases. The house, called Casteluzzo, and the surrounding countryside exceed all our expectations, and we settle in for a wonderful vacation.

Back in America, David is very envious, and he becomes more so when I call him every evening with an account of the day's adventures. Before the week's vacation is over, David and I have decided to return the following year. Again, we will bring a group of friends. Although we don't know it at the time, that vacation will lead to another one the year after that, and then another and another, sometimes twice a year, until without realizing it we are well on our way down that slippery slope some people call the "Italy thing."

Each time we return, it's always the same. On either side of the driveway, the sentinels attending us are cypress trees, rosemary, lavender, and rose bushes, all dutifully and aromatically welcoming us. There is fresh lemon cake, a bowl of just-picked figs, and a pitcher of rosemary and lavender on the table. In the orchard, plums and cherries are waiting to be picked. The local Orvieto Classico wine is waiting to be tasted. The sheep's-milk cheese of the area, called *pecorino*, is sweet and soft. Of course, we are in the countryside, and some country-style features can't be avoided. Crickets invade the house from time to time; the stove keeps running out of gas; our guests blow the lights with their hair dryers; the kitchen help needs a good shot of Right Guard. Our cell phones won't work inside the house because the walls, which are three feet of *tufa* block, deflect the signal, so we resort to hanging our phones in plastic bags out the window in order to receive calls. There is a small terracotta factory across the road that grinds away too early in the morning. But these problems only seem to add to the charm of Casteluzzo, and nothing can keep us from coming back year after year.

The house is, thankfully, "mouses"-free.

As a cookbook author, I am passionate about Italian food, and here is nature's bounty ready to be picked right outside the kitchen door—a cook's dream come true.

During our frequent visits, I fall into a routine. I take my friends to the weekly street market in the nearby town of Bagnoregio. I tell them to buy whatever they like, and we will see what we come up with for a meal that afternoon. I wait to see what my cooking lesson will be today as bent baskets of the harvested produce come into view, all spilling with red, yellow, green, and burgundy.

There is a cheese stand at the market offering a free bottle of wine if you buy a whole wheel of the local sweet *pecorino* cheese. Independently, two of us fall for this marketing ploy. One of our party drives our loot home while the rest of us walk home through the valley. On the way, we stop for a cool drink from a spring. Water gurgles from an old gargoyle's mouth set into the cliff face. The locals are there, too, filling containers with drinking water. There is a sign on the spring saying "*non potable,*" but someone has crossed this out. So you choose: *potable* or *non potable.* As all Italians do, I'll go with the locals rather than some official from Rome.

Back at the *casale,* I dispatch members of the team to the garden to gather herbs. They return with a fine selection, and some flowers too, a few peaches from the orchard, and smiles on their faces. I can see them still. When everything is settled, I hold an informal cooking lesson. My friends set to work on their market purchases and fresh-picked herbs. It turns out to be a meal to be reckoned with. No two meals are ever the same.

Rosemarie has made a fresh arugula salad that has a spicy taste like strong watercress. She chops in a fresh bulb of thinly sliced fennel that wafts of anise, and the Parmigiano Reggiano is crumbled onto the arugula and fennel. Just as she serves it, she drizzles it with some bright green, spicy Umbrian olive oil and some juice from a lemon picked from a nearby tree.

Tessa has gone to the *pasta fresca* shop and bought just-made linguine. She cooks the pasta for a few minutes, then chops thyme picked from near the rose bushes, mixes it with some purple cloves of garlic, and sprinkles it all with pine nuts. She borrows Rosemarie's olive oil and lemon juice to finish the dish.

Carole crossed the street to the butcher shop and purchases some spicy sausages. She picks large sprigs of rosemary to put under the sausages on the grill.

I buy an artist's palate of vegetables, red and green bell peppers, zucchini, scallions, eggplant, and fennel. I slice them at jaunty angles and toss them in a little olive oil too, and then put them on the grill with Carole's sausages and rosemary.

This joint effort takes no longer than thirty minutes from start to finish. We combine all this with some other wonderful purchases and pickings from the garden to make the menu below:

Arugula Salad with Parmesan and Fennel Tossed with Olive Oil and Lemon Juice (*recipe page 269)

Linguine Semplice with Thyme, Garlic, and Pine Nuts (*recipe page 303)

Grilled Sausages with Rosemary and Garlic (*recipe page 327)

Spicy Roasted Vegetables (fennel, bell peppers, zucchini, scallions, eggplant) (*recipe page 341)

Fresh Local Peaches and Grapes Right from the Vine

Little Lemon and Chocolate Tortas from the Bakery

Local Soft, Sweet Pecorino Cheese

Rosemary and Olive Bread from the Bakery

Limoncello, Grappa, and Vin Santo

The platters are carried out to the orchard, and we all gather round. The colors of the food splash on the terra cotta table. No one can wait for things to be served in order—we just eat it as it comes, and everything is heavenly. We are not too concerned with

27

polite manners, nor are we in much of a hurry to leave the table. It's a four-hour lunch, enjoying this enchanted food and the lively Orvieto Classico wine with the sun shining on us from a clear blue sky. I look around the table at the faces of my friends, who look as though they're six years old and Santa has just arrived.

❧

About four years into our "Italy rental thing" I'm once again on a day trip to Orvieto. Poor David is back in the USA, dealing with another corporate crisis. He is hoping to retire soon. I have come to Italy to spend a week with my brother and his family. I run into Signor Galli, the realtor. Elegant as ever, with his jacket still precariously perched on his shoulders, he is chatting with his friends outside his agency on Via del Duomo.

"*Come sta?*—How are you?" says dashing Signor Galli in his usual courtly manner.

"I hope you are enjoying your time back in Italy. You must like it here very much."

"Oh, yes. So much that perhaps I would like to buy a house here!" I reply on an impulse.

Galli responds with a broad smile and a torrent of Italian, which I understand to mean that he has at least ten houses in the area, any of which would suit me perfectly, and I should call at his office in the morning.

Chapter 6

It's a little awkward to back out now, and it might be fun just to see what there is to see. I present myself the next morning, ready to inspect the ten houses. I am excited as Signor Galli selects one of his impressive leather-bound albums of photographs, and starts to review them with me. This first house, he explains, is very nice, but already sold. The second house too. Don't even think about the next one—too many plumbing problems, and the one after that, the grandmother has died, so there will be problems with the heirs. The next one looks like one of the piles of rubble on his website, so I respectfully decline.

So it goes, and our excitement fades as we continue down the list. It turns out that only two of the ten houses are actually available to inspect, and neither of them are at all promising. One is a huge, run-down villa, which is going to take years to restore, and anyway, it is out of the question because this week he can't locate the *chiave*—key. The other is a small, one might almost say humble, dwelling in the middle of Lubriano. It doesn't seem worth the effort of going to see either of them.

I'm disappointed, which seems silly, as I'm not really in the market for a house; up until yesterday, I hadn't even thought about it. Still, once I start thinking about it, I have a feeling that something might magically come of it.

I call David back home in Denver and tell him that the whole exercise has been a failure. "What about the last house," he says, "the little place in Lubriano?"

I respond that after eliminating nine of our ten bright prospects, I am not going to see this small and obviously unsuitable house in the middle of Lubriano village. It will be a complete waste of time.

"Go see it," he says.

"No!" I repeat. "It will be a complete waste of time."

There is a short silence, and then he says, "You're on vacation, aren't you? So you have time. Go see it."

I can't think of a good rebuttal, so I find myself on the phone to Signor Galli, making arrangements to view the property.

I meet Signor Galli in front of the medieval entrance to the house. We inspect the property. It is not at all what I expected. It is old and quirky, with stairs going up and down on the outside to different levels. It has an arched entrance, a small courtyard, and a spacious garden (or what was once a garden) with what looks like a storage room or maybe a little cottage. The apartment consists of three bedrooms, a couple of small bathrooms, a kitchen with a huge fireplace, and a spacious living room. No room is perfectly square, but they are trying to be square.

I walk to the window of the *salone* and open the shutters. The view makes me catch my breath. The land falls away, plunging into the valley below, then, in the middle distance, an outcrop rises abruptly, a perfectly symmetrical hill. It is no more than a half-mile in front of my face, and it is crowned by the ancient and famous hill-top town of Civita di Bagnoregio.

We buy the place.

David buys it sight unseen; he is a very trusting soul. I buy it with just a fifteen-minute viewing. It takes a while to sink in that we have bought a home in a foreign country. Many of our friends, with thoughts of retiring too, are buying second homes in Arizona or Florida, and here we are buying a medieval dwelling in Europe. None of our friends can advise us on this crazy purchase. We are in this alone. We aren't sure whether we have done something incredibly clever or extremely foolish. All we are sure of is that we have bought an ancient dwelling in a far-off village where nobody speaks English. It is three long months before we are able to go back to Italy, view our purchase, and close the deal. Strangely enough, we never have buyers' remorse.

∽◦∾

Remorse or no remorse, while we wait for the closing, we have time to think over some of the things that we might have been smarter about. We contracted on the property after only one short look. We didn't look at any other properties, so we had nothing else to judge it by. We didn't counter-offer with a lower bid. We wonder if the locals are all laughing at us for buying the place. Come to think of it, we wonder how the locals will react to the arrival of two *stranieri*—foreigners—in their small and close-knit community. So it's with some trepidation that I return to Lubriano.

Our friends in the USA say "Where?" and we try to explain where Lubriano is. Not an easy question to answer, as the town doesn't appear on any of our maps. Luckily none of them ask, "Why?" That might be a harder question to answer.

In America, Lubriano would be dismissed as a one-horse town.

7

THIS IS A PALACE?

After the seemingly successful *atto* signing we have a flash of pride in ownership. I then realize that the house is not habitable until we can sift through Signora Morelli's leftovers. We are here with a few clothes and nothing else.

I take a walk along the single street that comprises the village of Lubriano. There is a large building on the main square. A small weathered sign says:"*Appartamenti/Matrimoni*"–Apartments/Weddings. I cautiously ring the bell. After a long pause, the door opens a few inches, and a young woman dressed in slippers peers out, rubbing her eyes.

"Can I help you?" she says in perfect English, making me realize I am not blending in here.

Overcoming my surprise, I explain our needs. She introduces herself as Gloria and informs us with an air of some importance that we are standing at the entrance of the Palazzo Monaldi. I must look dubious. This is a palace, this rather shabby-looking building right opposite the church?

Gloria explains that she works for the owners and that they have a few studio apartments, on the lower level of course. The palace proper starts one floor up above on the *piano nobile*. Her attitude is superior, but her clothing definitely is not.

Richard and I look. The apartments are obviously not used much, and they are a little faded. But they are only a hundred yards from our home, and I have the feeling that proximity is better than luxury. This will have to be home for a couple of weeks. We agree and pay up front. This will just have to do. Tomorrow we will check into the small studio apartment and try to make ourselves comfortable, ignoring the musty smell, dusty drapes, and general dinginess.

As we are leaving, we see Gloria running after us, asking us please to come back for a minute.

"Please to come and look at a more suitable accommodation."

I am not sure if it was my sideways look at the dusty drapes or Richard's large shoulders and feet that prompted this offer.

"A small apartment, Signora, I don't think it is enough."

She takes us to a spacious apartment with cheery windows looking onto the square. This view should help overcome my general feeling that I need to get to work and scrub this "palace," which consists of two bedrooms, a pleasant *salone*, pricey antiques begging for polish, and frescoes on the walls. We protest that this is quite unnecessary—it's too extravagant, and it's beyond our budget.

Gloria looks confused for a moment, and then brightens up. "No problem," she explains. "You have paid, Signora!"

We try to explain that we've paid for a modest studio, not this large suite of rooms, but she'll have none of it. Our protests are met with the oddly irrefutable logic that an apartment is an apartment.

"But you have paid, there is nothing more, Signora! We will expect you *domani!*"

I didn't know then, although I would find out soon enough, that Gloria was to be an important player in our new Italian life.

"Come get me if you need me, Signora!" Gloria calls out after me as we walk away, "You have found yourself in a four-cat town!" she adds. "The town is talking, Signora. What is an *Americana* doing buying a house here? Only Italians live here. There are no *stranieri* here!"

Precisely.

8

ATTENTI AI PROTESTANTI

With the key to our home in our possession, we can now relax. After dinner, Richard and I walk down to the local bar in Lubriano for an espresso and a brandy before heading off for bed. In Italy, a local bar or *caffe* is a blend of many things: it is a bar, a breakfast bar, a coffee bar, and a gelato shop in summer. But most importantly, it is the epicenter for village gossip. It is frequented by all, including young children. Village posters are displayed here, and the bar owner is often a walking internet search engine.

Across the valley, the lights on the footbridge to the town of Civita look like a string of pearls strung in the night sky. As we walk down the street, our footsteps echo in the silence of the town.

We look out of place. This is not a place where tourists—or, in fact, any non-Italian may stray. All is very still and calm; water trickles out of the cherub's urn in the village fountain and just a few lights shine behind medieval windows. A cat glides off into a shadow.

Warmed by coffee and brandy, we stroll back. Richard returns to our temporary home to work on his novel. As I enter the square, the church bells start ringing, calling to an imperceptible congregation.

The lights are dim inside this church. The only light is on the altar and the priest is slowly pacing up and down, silhouetted, throwing a shadow over the altar. On this chilly February night about thirty women and three men are sitting wrapped up in their warm winter coats, scarves wrapped around heads and throats. A few more elderly ladies arrive and, despite their age, genuflect deeply. The bells sound again and a young lady rushes past me, up the aisle and to the altar. Her shoes go *clacketeee* in the stillness of the church. She genuflects too and flops down like a rag doll in front of the organ. Thirty seconds later, the music begins.

Large velvet curtains are drawn over the church door, and I notice a gas heater on a side aisle. Its heat is making no impact on the chill of the church. The priest walks up to the altar, kneels down on a skimpy kneeler, and crouches forward so that his head almost touches the ground in front of him. He keeps this position for one and a half hours while he conducts the service.

He is probably in his mid-seventies. When he finishes the service, I'm quite sure he will stagger as he uncurls himself from this abject position. But he doesn't. At the closing he elegantly unfurls himself and stands bolt upright without so much as a waver. He rises up, turns around, and that is the end of the service.

You would think I had been at a nightclub, the way Richard looks at me when I walk in.

"Where *were* you?" he says in an accusatory fashion. "Church couldn't have gone on *that* long!"

"Want to bet?" I retort. "Why not ask the priest's knees?"

The phone rings in our "palace" apartment. It's our new neighbors, complaining that our shutters are banging and it is disturbing them. I have no idea how they know that we are staying here, but as Richard says, the whole town probably knows who we are and exactly what we are doing.

The bells sound all night across the square. I wonder how many masses that priest has said and how many hours he spent kneeling in that submissive position. Gloria says that she will get the priest to come and bless the house as soon as Signor Armstrong arrives. I doubt that the priest will be up for blessing the house of *Protestanti*. Gloria adds that Don Luigi is a "mystic." I'm not sure what this means, but the bottom line is that he is not super-friendly to these oddball American interlopers into his parish.

My bed in Palazzo Monaldi is about a hundred

feet from the church bell, which rings on the quarter hour. It's a relief when it gets to 1 a.m.—12:45 a.m. is a long haul, with twelve deafening clangs and three little dings.

Richard and I wake up the next morning to a fog suspended in the valley below. It is slowly rolling up and into the streets.

"Beware of these mists," Gloria warns us as she draws on a cigarette. It is hard to get out of bed and begin our restoration of who knows what.

9

SCRATCHING THE SURFACE

Scratching could not make it worse!
(Shakespeare, The Merchant of Venice*)*

"La Donna Mobile" rings from my new Italian cell phone. It's Gloria, calling from Palazzo Monaldi. She explains to me, in her smoky voice, that she and her husband Mario "job share" at the Palazzo, and she needs more than half a job and please she needs the money and do we have any work for her?

During our stay at the palace Gloria has proved herself to be as resourceful as the Artful Dodger. Every question we ask she has an answer for. She is street smart. Want a phone? No problem.

"But Gloria, we can't get a phone until we have certificates of residence!"

"No problem!" says Gloria, who calmly arranges for a phone for us in her name. We can transfer it later, she tells us.

Everything is "No problem!"

She translates, helps us install our computer, finds a plumber; she is a gem when it comes to matters Lubriano.

"I am from the streets of Manila, you know," Gloria tells us.

Her father died when she was six. Her mother left her in Manila and came to Italy as an immigrant worker, married an Italian, and settled in Italy. When Gloria was seventeen, her Italian stepfather adopted her and brought her to Italy to be reunited with her mother. She has a "don't mess with me" look about her.

Italians can be pretty racist, and make no secret of it, either. Filipinos are low on their list; Gloria knows it and is not going to let them get away with it.

Within an hour of being hired, Gloria starts cleaning. She arrives at the door with cappuccinos in hand for us. She also brings some Umbrian Lemon Cake that she has made. The cake is bright yellow, colored by fresh eggs and freshly grated lemon rind. She brings her two small sons with her.

Her four-year-old son Marco asks if I'm the cousin of the Virgin Mary. I am so unlike anything he has seen before, he says, all fair skin and pink. He says I have fair hair and blue eyes just like Elizabeth, the cousin of the Virgin Mary in his book at school. He is quite convinced of this fact. I'll use my power wisely. He tells his mother that she better work hard because I could give very good references.

We are daunted by the work that needs to be done in the house, especially in the kitchen. So we ignore it. I feel as though I have just given a dinner and am leaving the dishes in the sink and going to bed. Instead we begin to clean out the little cottage in the back garden, which on our deed of sale is called an *annesso*. Starting here is ridiculous, but we tell ourselves we are beginning here because some of this junk in the *annesso* could be recycled for use in the house. Really, we are employing the technique of procrastination.

The little house has about fifty years of debris in it—debris ranging from old bottles for preserving, an old mirror, and some old chairs to a stack of long-playing records, about a hundred of them. These are all from one collection put out by a single company. It is an encyclopedia of music that contains all the classics. It's quite a thrill to find them, and I am sure David will enjoy seeing what is in this collection. David is in love with classical music. He is hoping to retire soon and spend many happy hours relaxing after a very hectic and successful career in the retail industry.

Amongst all the rubble and under broken tiles is an old gramophone, probably from the 1950s. I am not sure that this will be David's ideal method of musical appreciation. I can see him, rather, sitting in the *salone* in the house, gazing at Civita in the distance, the goddess looking down on him from the ceiling, listening to Beethoven's Fifth Piano Concerto, happy that I am sifting through piles of cast-offs and he is not.

I think this is called "division of labor." I have no complaints. Without his career, none of this would have been possible.

Signora Morelli told us at the closing that she had been born in the place she was just about to hand over to us. She and her sisters and cousins had all inherited the house, which she called a *palazzino*. Signor Galli told us that in the 1930s our garden was called *La Spia*—the spy. The family would sit in the garden and look down on their lands below, like royalty in the box at Wimbledon, watching the sweaty peasants. At that time the valley was filled with vines and olive trees, and they could keep a watch on their workers toiling away in the fields. Today no one works this land. We look down onto a fallow field below us, where a man is sitting with his wife. He has brought a table out into the middle of the fields there. And so we too spy on people. They are sitting there in silence. They have one irregular, dusty wheel of cheese stabbed with a rusty old knife, a loaf of bread, and a bottle of wine.

Beyond them, most of the valley is filled with trees. Gloria tells us that not a quarter of a mile away, further down the valley, a landslide has just occurred, exposing a wall of Etruscan dovecotes. This landslide has caused the bridge into Lubriano to become unstable, but no repair work can be done before the people from Antiquities are called in.

"With the Department of Antiquities involved that bridge will never get fixed, then Lubriano will be cut off as it always was before they built that bridge in the 1950s!" says Gloria, the harbinger once more.

I go into the house and decide to see if the gramophone works, so that I can tell David when he calls later that he has his work cut out for him in the form of listening to all the old records. The little gramophone works, and I wonder at the indistinct sound that comes out of it. I feel as though I am in the movie *Out of Africa* when Karen Blixen plays her old scratchy Danish gramophone for Finch-Hatton, who is just in from hunting lions. I feel like calling my friends and saying, "I have a home in Italy at the foot of the Calanchi Hills!"

I dust off some books, a set of old encyclopedias that were meant for *ragazzi*—the young. Studying these will help us to learn Italian.

Each day I dig a little deeper into this little *annesso*, hoping that a scorpion or snake doesn't come out from under the long-undisturbed dumping ground that this cottage has obviously been! There are so many old baked clay—*cotto*—tiles and so many screens and doors here that it's hard to count them. I can think of many ways to use them. I am sure some Morelli ancestors and maybe even some Jesuit monks are happy that I am not throwing this all away. An enormous black spider has his old, dusty web spun close to the window. His years here have been undisturbed. He gives me a proprietary look, and I open the window and hope he makes his own exit.

There is an alcove right by the fireplace in the kitchen, and when I sit in it I can see that it's a wonderful place to keep warm and see both doors into the kitchen at the same time. It's a safe haven. It's a refuge. I can feel the monks that have sat here before me. There are prayers in the walls.

There is also an extremely large old wine flagon with straw on the outside. It looks as though it would hold about 25 liters. This is apparently good to use for both wine and olive oil. That much wine is fine, but I think so much olive oil would not be an option. It's hard to imagine Signora Morelli, who lived on her own, consuming a flagon of either wine or olive oil. Perhaps this is the secret to her youthfulness.

My neighbor Signora Gaspari, in between a thousand other machine-gun-fired words, is saying "*Radice, radice!*" I think this means "roots." I think she is telling me something about the roots of one of the old Roman pines on our property. They appear to be interfering with her cantina, which is apparently dug underneath our garden. It may be the beginning of a long story. I think I should play it cool. I am taking a lesson from Barry Unsworth in his book *After Hannibal.* He says that in Italy, if a neighbor comes complaining about a problem and you go with him to look at it, this means that you are good as guilty and immediately become responsible for fixing it. I am sure that the Gasparis have been bugging Signora Morelli for years about the root problem, so they can wait a bit longer. Gloria says that root problems are usually difficult to resolve. Good fences make good neighbors; I am not sure how cantinas and Roman pines fit into this. It's a wonderful old tree that should have a string quartet sitting underneath it. It is the type of tree associated with Roman ruins, very tall and with a straight trunk holding up a huge green shady umbrella.

I give Signora Gaspari the "*Non capisco!*"—I don't understand—stock answer and save this problem for another day. Judging by her shrug and sigh, and the beginning of a mutter under her breath, I imagine the "another day" will probably be tomorrow.

Mario, Gloria's husband, appears on our doorstep today. He is from Naples. He has a winning smile, fiery black Moorish eyes, powerful shoulders, a rather large beer belly and a wild shock of black curly hair. He looks as though he should be a dock worker down on the bay in Napoli. He looks nothing like the short, stocky, fairer-skinned Umbrians who populate our town. I can imagine him immigrating to the USA and working in New York. He swaggers towards me as if to say "I take crap from no one." Gloria says that he is intensely proud of his Neapolitan ancestry. These people are noted for being hardworking but difficult. That looks like it is Mario through and through.

Just as Gloria becomes our self-appointed housekeeper, Mario appoints himself our handyman and gardener. He says he met Gloria when he was making pizzas in Rome near the Coliseum. He made her a pizza in the shape of a heart and put his phone number under it.

Within minutes of making a very loose arrangement for an hourly wage, should he be required to work for us at some time in the future, Mario is back at my doorstep with a chainsaw in hand. He is hell bent on trimming back the dense, overgrown garden. I let him start on an old wisteria that has a leg-thick arm which is creeping into and through the broken window of the *annesso*. The vine is pretty, but has not been trimmed in decades, I presume. He trims it back, hacking at it as though he is fleeing in a jungle. He cuts it back, in fact, much too far, which, I am sure, will place the vine in jeopardy. This vine I try to save in vain is referred to by Mario as "that vine that was going to destroy your foundations" and "that vine that you loved so much." As he leaves for the day, I offer him a large glass of red wine, which he downs in a few seconds. He salutes me and squeezes his eyes together with a smile on his face.

It seems we are to have a lot of "job sharing" going on here.

We name our home Braccioforte: *braccio* meaning "arm" and *forte* meaning "strong." It sounds so much better than Armstrong. Only later do we find out that this is actually a rather famous Italian name, but the name suits the solid fortress-type walls of the house, so with sincere apologies to the true Braccioforte family we stick with it.

We settle in to feel the pulse of the village; friends come and go from the USA to see our purchase, which at this stage is little more than an empty shell. Spring slides into summer. Braccioforte is little more than a base work camp for restoration and for learning the Italian language, irregular verbs and all.

10

MAIN STREET, LUBRIANO

Better a row of shopkeepers than a den of thieves,
Better a string of camels than a swarm of bees!
(Ethiopian proverb)

The one and only street in Lubriano slides along the crest of the hill. Cliffs plunge down into the valley on either side of it. It is called Via Roma. Why Via Roma? No one seems to know. Despite its grand name, it is a modest thoroughfare, no more than a lane. The cobbled street is exactly nine feet wide, with no sidewalks and no front gardens. Very little traffic passes our door, but the little that does rushes by at true Italian speed, almost brushing the walls as it passes. When leaving our front door it is advisable to carefully poke your head out first and check that the coast is clear, before cautiously extending your foot out as if you are going to swim in a very cold swimming pool.

All along Via Roma, the houses lean against each other, following the gradual, almost imperceptible curves of the street in one meandering old row. The sunlight slants into the lane, bringing to life the colors of the old buildings, each one aged to a soft tone of its former glory. The dusty colors, pink, brown, and gold textured into each other, tug at you like a sunset. The old iron street lamps, flower boxes, window shutters, and balconies turn every house into an idealized vision of a village in Italy. Everything is perfect—so picturesque that I worry that it may one day, if it is ever "discovered," come to look like a cliché of what it should be.

As you enter Lubriano from the main road, a small square opens before you protected by chestnut trees. There is a small fountain, a drop-dead view over the Calanchi valley, and a small war memorial in the middle. The names on the memorial are the names of this town—Gaspari, Manzotti, Rocchi, Morelli—the fathers, grandfathers, and even the children of Lubriano. With a pang I realize that, even in this peaceful and lovely place, war and death have taken their toll, and that even Italy, so lovely and so joyful, has had and will have its dark days too.

The square is called the Col di Lana, the Square of the Wool. In days before, the sheep from the valley below were assembled for shearing here at the entrance to the town. Beneath the chestnut trees, next to the town pump, there are one or two benches, always used by the proverbial four old men, who are a fixture in every small Italian town. Day after day they sit there, conducting muttered conversations and eyeing any would-be entrants into the town. Nothing goes unnoticed; no newcomer escapes scrutiny. The villagers observe all who arrive, all who leave, and any variation in the well-established rhythms in the daily life of Lubriano.

The narrow street with its buildings squeezed one on top of the other threads its way from the Col di Lana to the town square. There, the Church of John the Baptist sits comfortably beside the Palazzo of the Monaldi, the ruling family of this area in feudal times. I reflect again that this is truly Italy, where the church and the nobility have ruled side-by-side for centuries, sometimes peacefully, more often in an uneasy alliance, and sometimes in open hostility to each other. Beyond the palazzo the street goes on through the oldest part of the town, past sleeping houses and sleeping cats, until it peters out at the *cimitero*, the cemetery, the ultimate dead end.

Shops here bear no signs. Anna, the hairdresser, snips away all day in an anonymous shop not ten feet by ten feet, while all inside are engulfed in a towering mound of the equivalent of *People* magazines. When I tip her for a good hair cut, she, not knowing the

English for "cheap," draws her fists quickly into her midriff to describe the usual tip of nothing from the locals.

Luigina needs no advertising for her *Frutta e Verdure,* where the imperfect fruit and vegetables of the village are sold in the front of her shop and the pretty and perfect ones shipped in are relegated to the back of the store. "Just picked" here means just that. Huge braids of garlic are the only standard fixture here; they make swags along with photos of Padre Pio. All the produce changes with the season to reflect what the *contadini* have brought in to be sold.

Strolling along Via Roma, I notice a tiny pedestrian alley with shallow steps and tunneled underneath someone's balcony. This balcony, like all the balconies on the main street, is the Italian substitute for a dryer. Flapping there like flags is someone's ample underwear. Sunshine wins out over privacy. The little alley below has the name Vicolo Morelli. Signora Morelli said it was named for her cousin, who was killed by the Germans in World War II. It seems believable.

In the evening, the town takes on a somewhat split personality. The Admiral Bar, or *caffe,* at one end is filled with the young, who flaunt tight jeans, noisy motorcycles, and various pierced body parts. The *caffe* is brightly lit, in contrast to the dim village lanterns. As I walk by, I think of Ernest Hemingway and his short story "A Clean, Well-Lighted Place." The mood of this bar matches the mood of that story; it is functional and sometimes remote, with an inability to see the world at large.

The street begins here and leads, as if through time, to the other end of town. At the other end the old-timers live peacefully with their friends and their memories. It ends at the cemetery, dark and silent. In the peaceful light of day, widows and widowers walk quietly down this street, carrying armfuls of flowers to lay on the graves of their spouses. They make the cemetery an extension of the life of the village rather than a dead end.

Wake up early and you will see workers heading for the fields with scythes or hoes on their shoulders. Wake a little later and you will see women on shopping expeditions, friends congregating at particular chosen spots along the road. In winter there are warm spots where the sun's rays angle between the buildings to soothe chilled bones. In summer there are cool spots where a fresh breeze steals between the houses baking together in a tight row. Up and down our old Via Roma, this is our street. Women sit on tiny stools, chatting quietly as they strip fennel seeds from the plants they have brought in from the fields. This is slow, tedious work, done patiently as their mothers and grandmothers did it before them. I watch in fascination, and promise myself that, when cooking with fennel seed in the future, I'll remember these ladies and recall that the collection of a teaspoon of fennel seeds equals an hour of manual labor.

A permanent fixture in the village is an old man, with sad eyes, unshaven and clothes unwashed. Up and down, up and down, back and forth on Via

Roma he goes. His dog walks alongside him, a long chain dragging on the ground, chinking, chinking along the street. I ask Gloria about this melancholy old man, and she says he is a small farmer who has been abandoned by his family and lives alone with his dog on the edge of town. A week later she comes back with an apology.

"Signora, I told you wrong. He is not a farmer."

"Then what does he do?" I ask.

"Oh, he is a drunkard" she says.

"But what does he do?"

She looks puzzled for a moment, and then breaks into a smile as she understands my question. "That's what he does, Signora. He is a drunkard."

Although I am fairly certain that this is not a recognized profession, even in laid-back Lubriano, I decide not to pursue this particular line of conversation any further.

I am surprised to see that there are two butchers in town. This seems an improbable luxury for such a small place. One of my new neighbors murmurs to me confidentially that I should patronize the one closer to us. The owners buy everything directly from a local *fattoria,* and everything that they sell in the butcher shop is sure to be fresh. She whispers that the other butcher shop is suspected of purchasing some of their meat from (horror of horrors) a wholesaler!!!

I take her advice and visit the recommended one. The shop is spotless, with an amazing selection. Pork, beef, chicken and turkey are laid out before me, not to mention a number of different salamis and sausages. The butcher shop purchase takes quite a long while. There are usually four or five of us waiting, all local ladies. The village ethos does not yet approve of men folk getting involved in anything as domestic as butcher purchases. As I wait patiently with my neighbors in the butcher shop, we chat away idly. All the village gossip is passed around, and nobody is in any hurry.

The owner, Giuseppina, is a lovely lady with a scrubbed smile, velvety smooth skin, rosy cheeks, and blue eyes. Her white coat and cap are starched and gleaming, making her eyes look bluer still. She always wears high heels. She tells me that she likes our son. She says that he is *simpatico*, and I agree. She tells me that everyone in the village has noticed him because he is so big and tall and everyone is saying that it is nice to have him here in their village. I tell her that I like her teenage daughter and that she and her daughter look like sisters. She blushes. Her husband is grappling, a little grumpily, in the back room with a length of *salsicce*. The long rope of sausage is coiled as though ready to attach to an anchor on the wharf.

Giuseppina begins working on my order. Everything is done by hand; it's inconceivable that anything could be prepackaged. She handles my order for six quail as though they are pieces of jewelry, lovingly placing them on the wax paper, and wrapping each of these gems individually. I will cook them as I always do: I stuff them with garlic and rosemary and place them in a chestnut roaster, charring them directly over the fire. There is a pleasant smoky flavor when quail is cooked this way (*recipe page 323).

Giuseppina then starts on my *spiedini*—kebabs. Each piece of meat is carefully cut to size, mushrooms and peppers are added, and finally the finished products are laid before me for approval. Next, she proudly hacks off a huge piece of well-aged Chiana steak for me. I will cook it on the bone to make *Bistecca Fiorentina* (*recipe page 335). I will char it, tied with rosemary, over very hot coals. It's a quick, delicious, and much-appreciated main course; it costs an awful lot of money if you order it in a Florentine restaurant!

The busiest day of the week in the butcher shop is Friday. Seemingly in defiance of the Catholic tradition of fish on Friday, a whole deboned pig is laid out on a giant slab of marble. This is an Italian traditional dish called *Porchetta* (*recipe page 331). Giuseppina's husband stuffs the unfortunate porker with a highly aromatic stuffing of sage, onion, and fennel and roasts him on a spit. On Friday morning at opening time, Giuseppina will hang up the "*Porchetta*" sign, announcing a pig roast Italian-style. The wafts of roasted *porchetta* lead you to the butcher shop, and she will slice the pig into delectable rounds for you, with a rich crust of honey-colored crackling on the outside and the aromatic dressing in the middle.

My son Richard is of the opinion that the *porchetta* made in Rome, stuffed with rosemary, is superior, but in our region it's always stuffed with sage, onion, and fennel, and I would be very hesitant about suggesting to a Lubrianese that the Roman version might be in any way preferable. Richard is a food aficionado. In our family we have two camps; my husband, son Anthony, and daughter Heather are all in Camp C.P.A., and Richard and I are in Camp "English Majors and Passionate Cooks" (E.M.P.C.s). It is good to have Richard along to talk about the Italian novel while we are appreciating the fruits of an Italian table.

On a Saturday morning the butcher shop is filled to capacity. Some *porchetta* remains available, and weekend residents of the village are buying in bulk in order to stock their larders in Rome. Everyone is happy to join in the village gossip exchanged here.

There is the tobacconist shop called the *Sale e Tabacchi.* We must back up to medieval times and the story of Italy and salt. Ancient salt monopolies entitled salt to be sold only through the Italian government, so for hundreds of years salt was only sold at the tobacconist, who acted as agents for the ruler of the moment. That is the *Sale* in *Sale e Tabacchi.* The *Tabacchi* part involves large quantities of cigarettes, which are sold in a vending machine outside the store entrance to anyone of any age (mostly the young) who wishes to purchase the dreadful things.

Bruno is the owner. He is from the Amalfi Coast and moved up to Lubriano for a business opportunity. He is usually in a hurry, unlike his Lubrianese shopkeeper counterparts. His store is set into what on first appearance looks like the opening to a Roman tomb. Right here, the old retired school teacher points to the jagged remains of an old wall.

"This was a battlement and the ancient *porta*"—gate—"into the village. In 1920, they knocked down the city wall, which was built around 1600, to allow trucks to enter the village," he says disparagingly.

Bruno also has the village responsibility for twenty-first century communications. He has a fax machine and a computer and can add minutes onto your cell phone. Give him your phone number and Euro 50, and thirty seconds later you have Euro 50 open to call on your *telefonino*. This present-time situation stops for the month of August, when Bruno's parents come into town to take over running the shop while Bruno is on vacation. Medieval techniques then apply, and the mere mention of sending a fax is enough to get you thrown out of the store.

I wander back to the Piazza San Giovanni Battista just before lunch. There is a mobile fish shop on the square. Apparently the seafood has come from the Adriatic. I pick out four very large *gamberi*—prawns—and walk back home to grill them fiercely on top of the stove with a little lemon juice, olive oil, garlic, and rosemary. I press them down firmly with a spatula so that the shells became caramelized and crusty. They are divine (*recipe page 313).

All the local shops are supplemented by frequent trucks that come through the town selling their wares. While Italians are fanatical about air pollution, sound pollution does not seem to worry them. Regularly each morning, with deafening regularity, some sort of truck comes through town. Each one is equipped with the worst fog-horn scratchy megaphone you could impossibly imagine. It makes me feel as though I am in World War II and the Nazis are invading the town; it's startling and disconcertingly loud. The words sound as scratchy and incoherent as they do coming through an American fast food drive-through. Some trucks sell flowers, others fruit, and of course there is the welcome fish truck from the Adriatic. Trucks even come through blaring that they are selling space-age kitchens to fit into medieval dwellings.

The occasional itinerant comes through town selling wares and the word is soon spread around: *Stranger in town, stranger in town.* People peep out suspiciously through shutters.

I see Luigina from the fruit and vegetable shop walking out of the bakery with a roasting pan. In it is a roasted goose, with a deep brown crust and caramelized onions (*recipe page 325). She puts the roasting pan in the trunk of her car and brings out a carving knife and fork. I am unsure what is happening. She carves a large piece of the breast onto a plate, throws some onions around it, slams the trunk closed, and waves enthusiastically at me to wait as she bolts up a narrow flight of stairs. One minute later I am still standing there at the trunk, mad for the rich, brown holiday aroma seeping through the trunk. She is soon back and explains that the bakery will let you roast anything in the oven after the morning baking session is over. *Buoni*—excellent beyond description—she tells me, describing the deep heat of a baker's oven. She has just taken some goose to an old, immobile aunt before whisking it home to her dinner table.

A few yards further along the street, the shoemaker is bent over someone's old shoe. They say he has been a fixture on Via Roma for many years with his tiny *calzoleria*—shoemaker's shop. His seventy or more years of cobbling shoes have probably taught him patience and acceptance, and he looks like an old worn shoe himself, with his placid face, stooped shoulders, and big, skillful hands. In medieval times his workshop would have been a storage cellar, and it's still as small, dark, and uncomfortable as it probably was then.

One day he is not sitting huddled in his usual position, but is rather sitting out on the side of the street, surrounded by a group of locals. He is covered from head to toe in white bandages and plaster casts. He looks like a cartoon character, so swathed in bandages is he. He is perched on an old chair, with one of his legs sticking out into the narrow street, rigid in its huge cast, creating an immediate danger that a passing car could break it again. I stop to express sympathy and ask what happened. While I am trying to understand his country accent, Gloria strolls by and helpfully translates for me.

"It is pruning time, and he fell out of the top of a fruit tree. Broke a lot of bones," she says, somewhat impatiently.

"But Gloria, he's nearly ninety years old. What on earth is he doing climbing trees at his age?"

"Like I said, Signora, it's pruning time. This is the countryside. These things happen."

"Well, at least his friends are worried about him."

"Oh, yes, Signora. All the villagers wish him long life. Not many shoemakers left in village Italy. Big problem if he dies."

And with this unsympathetic explanation, she goes on her way.

A month or two later he is back at work in his Pinocchio-sized workshop. Enough of his dressings have been removed to enable him to function. Looking for an opportunity to give him some business, I take a suitcase to him to repair. It has suffered from the blows of some overzealous airline baggage handlers.

He looks at it doubtfully. A difficult job, it will take a few days. When I pick it up, he presents his bill for the princely sum of three dollars. Despite my protestations that he is cheating himself, he will not take a penny more. Still trying to be a good customer, I bring him a pair of shoes to mend. This time the price is zero, and includes delivering the repaired shoes to my door. Reluctantly I realize that my efforts to help his business seem to be having precisely the opposite effect, so I tell him that the price for all future work must be agreed before the job is started. This puts me in the curious position of haggling with a shopkeeper to get him to raise his prices.

There is a quaint little *ristorante* at the edge of Main Street called *Vecchio Mulino*, The Old Mill. The owner is Giuseppe, and he is a Tuscan. He married a Lubriano lady some thirty-five years ago, but in this town he is still a Tuscan. Like all Tuscans, he is immensely proud of his heritage, but the villagers, on the other hand, don't much care what he is, since he is not Lubrianese and never will be.

The dining room is quite small and cramped, with pink walls of a Pepto Bismol shade and a few photographs of the flood in Florence twenty years ago rounding out the decor. There is no view, because there are no windows. The kitchen is even more cramped, occupied by a small stove and a large cook. In marked contrast to the dining room, the kitchen boasts a sizeable window, with a spectacular view over the Calanchi valley.

He serves a soup called *Carabaccia* (*recipe page 281), and our friends who visit us all become hooked on it. The best compliment that you can give a chef in Italy to describe a wonderful dish is to twist your finger on your cheek. This soup is finger-to-the-cheek good. Giuseppe always responds with a smile. We are such regulars that we notice that Giuseppe always wears the same sweater, and his restaurant is just like him—old, comfortable, and a bit worn out. At the sight of us stepping through the beaded curtain at his front door he brings out a bowl of *Carabaccia*. This is a *casseruola* more than a soup; it is mostly onions and peas but has celery and carrots in it too. For good measure, the chef bakes an egg onto the top of the soup. I have read that Catharine de Medici took this recipe to France, creating the basis for French onion soup. It is slow-roasted, with a labor-intensive stock so rich and flavorful that it would be hard to replicate in a time-constrained American kitchen. This dish is so perfect that we order it time after time, feeling a bit guilty that we are so unimaginative that we seldom try anything else. When we do summon up the energy to step off the well-worn *Carabaccia* track, we usually order *Pappardelle al Cinghiale* (*recipe page 291). Its dense rich sauce of wild boar simmering in red wine wafts a gutsy and earthy aroma. It will be served on top of *Pappardelle*, the pasta of the region, thin, flat, and about one inch wide, and the perfect partner for this serious sauce. It is cooked for hours, and the lovely reduction warms you right through.

During the slow process of getting our food we start chatting to the couple at the next table, a rather dashing Italian man and his English wife. We learn that they live in a villa near Lubriano, and we are happy that we are on to the next level of acquaintances. Clateo is retired from Alitalia and has lived in every part of the world. He is very dissatisfied at having retired to live near Lubriano. He really would prefer to live in England, but his English wife will have none of it. We too are a bit puzzled by his ambition. One is always meeting Englishmen who want to retire to sunny Italy, but Italians who pine for a life in chilly England are a distinctly rare breed. Our new friend tells us with disdain that everything in Italy is crazy. Someone is building a totally illegal house right opposite City Hall, the airport in Milan is a big political scam, and all foreigners in Italy are taken advantage of; it's all crazy. Without our realizing it, he thereupon appoints himself as our advisor, savior, and general protector against all the ills with which Italy is sure to assail us.

Clateo's wife Cecily is frightfully posh, and talks as though she has a hot potato in her mouth. She is quite elegant, supermodel thin, has a bob of fair hair and a deep tan, and wears a white linen dress. She keeps on nipping out of the restaurant for a cigarette. She adds comments by sticking her head back through the restaurant door. Words filter through puffs of smoke.

"My God!" she says. "England is positively dreadful, and the people are a pain in the arse."

While we wait for our food, the wine is passed around, and in one short hour, our new friend Clateo, who clearly has one foot in our old world and two feet in our new world, proceeds to give us a lesson on the vagaries and injustices of the Italian medical system, the absurdities of the legal system, and the peculiarities of the community at large. Everyone in Lubriano, Clateo explains with a chuckle, is a little crazy. He taps his forehead meaningfully. All these people have lived too long in these old houses, built from volcanic *tufa* rock. And what is the result? It's obvious. It has made them crazy. There is radiation in the *tufa*, and the radiation has got to them. That explains why they are all crazy.

He sits back, satisfied that he has made his point, and he is certainly convincing. Every sentence is emphasized with pleading fingertips and expressive eyes.

Chapter 10

"You must understand that *thees* is Italy," he says frequently to drive home his points.

His wife returns to the table and sits quietly, firmly shut up, sometimes shaking her head, and sometimes rolling her eyes. I think she has been down this road before. She may disagree with some of his more forceful opinions, but an Italian who wants to live in England must be given some space, some respect. Or, at least, must be humored!

Our food starts to arrive, first one entree, then a few minutes later a second one, then a salad, followed by a vegetable dish, then another entree, and so on. There seems to be no organization to the meal, but it's amazing what you will put up with when the food is all so incredibly flavorsome. No apologies are made—you either take it or leave it—but it's worth the strange system the cook has constructed. She is probably distracted by the incredible view of Civita rising out of the valley in front of her, and of course she is constrained by the capacity of her little stove. We wait patiently in the dining room, entertaining ourselves with the Pepto-Bismol decor. We have ordered side vegetables and they come well after we have finished everything else, but they are worth waiting for. Crispy fried Swiss chard; tiny, crusty rosemary potatoes; and wonderful *fagioli*—Tuscan beans cooked with garlic and drizzled with the local bright green olive oil and a little lemon juice. We are vaguely aware that in any other restaurant we would not be pleased with the haphazard delivery of our different courses, but here it seems to add to our feeling of satisfaction in finding ourselves in such a happy place.

Again and again we return to Giuseppe's for the luscious food and the simple ambience. It seems to capture perfectly the essence of our new Italian life. How could we have guessed that Giuseppe would teach us all a lesson, and that darker days lay just ahead? Main Street never stays the same.

11

THE EMPRESS STRIKES BACK

Will Neptune's ocean wash clean my hand?
(Lady Macbeth)

The character of the Morelli family is coming more clearly into focus, and it's not, as they say, a pretty picture. After the dramas of the closing on our property, we thought that we would have no more dealings with them. But no such luck. In fact, Signora Morelli's brother pays us what you would not describe as a social call. I turn around and there he is, standing in the entrance to my *salone*, having walked in uninvited and without so much as a knock at the door. I demand to know what he is doing in my house, he casually announces that he has come to take his sister's lawnmower. He then skips out of the house and hoists the ancient machine under his arm.

By now, I have had enough experience with the customs and laws of Italy to know the rules for a situation like this. When you sell a house, you can take all the movables with you, (and the Morellis had a pretty liberal interpretation of what comprised movables!) but anything you leave behind becomes the property of the new owner. Usually it's no more than a lot of throwaway items, with possibly a few odds and ends of some value. In our case, we had certainly inherited piles of chucked out items, and virtually nothing of any value. But now, Signor Morelli tells me, via the kind translation of Gloria, that he considered it his right to come by and remove whatever belonged to his sister, and he didn't think it necessary to ask our permission. He says it with no apologies; he sees it as his right to do whatever he wants, unconstrained by either law or custom.

Our friend Peter, the English lawyer living in Italy, had solemnly advised us to change all the locks on the first day after the signing of the *atto*, and now it is clear that he was right. Gloria and Mario are horrified at the gall of this man. Without even telling me, they rush off right away to the neighboring village to buy new locks for both the front and back doors. Gloria is furious; she walks out of our door shaking her head and her fist at the same time.

There is no stopping these people, I think. I decide that I will let him take the lawnmower, since I don't need it (for at this stage we have no lawn), but it is time to take my stand. I march up to him, and standing less than a foot from his nose, I shake my finger in his face and yell, "*BASTA*—ENOUGH! Get out!"

He looks at me with alarmed astonishment, and then hurries off with the lawnmower. If I hadn't been so annoyed I would probably have found something amusing in the sight of this distinguished-looking man scurrying down our front stairs with a rusty vintage lawnmower under his arm. He is trying to look nonchalant and carrying it as though it were as light as a balloon. I think he gets the message, but as soon as Gloria and Mario return, we change all the locks.

We decide that we must put an end to these intrusions, and we need local help, so we call Clateo, who had kindly offered us his help when we met him recently at Giuseppe's local restaurant. We call his home, a villa in the countryside a few miles away.

"Well, *dahling*" says Cecily, "he's not here at the moment. In fact, he's in Lubriano."

We ask if we should call back later.

"Call back?" says Cecily. "Why do you want to do that? He's already in Lubriano. Just pop your head out of the window and you're sure to see him pass by."

This singular contact system seems to work, because sure enough, a few minutes later, Clateo saunters past, jingling his car keys and cutting a dashing figure with his crop of white hair, tanned complexion, dark glasses, and white linen shirt. We call down to him, asking if he'd like some tea. He acts as though this chance encounter is no coincidence at all. We tell him about our problems with the Morellis as we sit under the fig tree, sipping some tea and then a glass or two of *Vin Santo* too.

Clateo gets very angry and red in the face when we tell him what has happened. He confides that it would have been much better if we had never bought our house from the Morellis. If he had met us earlier, he would never have allowed such a thing to happen. The bad reputation of the Morellis is widespread. In fact, Clateo says that our neighbor Signora Gaspari has been warning prospective buyers against buying our place for years by telling them about the problems they will inherit with the house. She has been cautioning all interested parties not to buy the home from these crafty tricksters.

After deep consideration of our situation, Clateo suggests that we write a letter to Signor Morelli to demand that he never set foot in Braccioforte again. Better yet, he says, make it a registered letter. Come to think of it, we should send it with guaranteed delivery, too. Oh yes, and better demand it be delivered with receipt confirmation required, to make sure it was received by him. Otherwise he will never admit to having received such a letter. By this time our heads are spinning with the complexities of sending a simple letter, but Clateo disagrees. He sits back, feeling pretty good about this solution, although he is still a little concerned that he may have overlooked some level of confirmation, certification, guarantee, or other formality that would make our letter strike the maximum level of fear into the recipient.

But we feel we don't have time for all this maneuvering and foreplay, and we don't think that the annoying Signor Morelli would pay the slightest attention to a mere letter from anyone, much less a couple of upstart foreigners with no local connections. So we tell Clateo that we are thinking about going to see our lawyer, as we feel that we had better nip this problem in the bud. Clateo is horrified at the very idea.

"A lawyer?" he says in disbelief. "Why go see a lawyer?"

Clateo has lawyers pegged alongside a large cast of other swindling devils, including most professions, businessmen, the Italian government, and, for that matter, Italians in general, especially if they're from the South.

"He will charge you *un sacco di soldi*—a sack of money—to handle this matter," he says. "And then he still won't fix the problem. A lawyer! Ha ha! Might just as well go to the police!"

Clateo chuckles heartily at this last idea, as though the thought of going to the police is beyond ridiculous. We decide not to mention that it was one of the remedies we were considering! We are sorry we pushed Clateo's button on the lawyer thing. We promise to think it over for a few days, but secretly we have already decided to go and see our lawyer anyway. If nothing else, it will give us an opportunity to spend a day in Bolsena, where Dr. Ricci has his office. It's one of our favorite towns, and only about ten miles from Lubriano.

The road winds along the crest of a hill, with marvelous views over the bright blue waters of Lake Bolsena; it turns under the forbidding walls of the Monaldi fortress (the Monaldis seem to have built a fortress or palace in every town in these parts), and then drops steeply into the town of Bolsena. It is a place we love, a beautiful little town hardly known outside this area, with its own little climate zone, sheltered from the winter winds by its cliffs and tempered by the deep blue waters of the lake.

When it is a little warmer, we usually come here to lunch on Bolsena's *Corregone.* This type of trout was introduced not too long ago and has flourished in the lake. Many lakeside restaurants grill it with rosemary, olive oil, and butter (*recipe page 315) and serve it with Rosemary Roasted Potatoes (*recipe page 343). But today is not the day for *Corregone!*

History is everywhere in Bolsena. Even in a country like Italy, where thousands of years of history are piled on top of each other, this barely known little town is a very special place. The Etruscans built a major center here around 400BC, and the Romans pushed them out 500 years later. The amazing ruins of these great civilizations are easy to find on the outskirts of the town, although hardly anybody goes to see them. In the center of the town is an ancient church, with Christian catacombs under its walls. The church, dedicated to Santa Christina, is old—not just old, but beyond our comprehension, dating from around 300 AD.

For about a thousand years, the church went

about its business, undisturbed by the outside world, but in the year 1263, the great miracle of Bolsena occurred, and that changed everything. This miracle is the subject of the Roman Catholic feast day of Corpus Christi (in Italy, the feast day is called Corpus Domini).

A priest from Prague on his pilgrimage to Rome was taking communion at the altar of the ancient church of Santa Christina when the wafer in his hand started to spill blood onto the altar cloth. Thus began Corpus Christi. This miracle reverberated around all Italy, and was held up by the Church as proof positive that the doctrine of transubstantiation had been proven beyond doubt. The Pope, Urban IV, was ecstatic, and decreed that a mighty cathedral be constructed to house the relics of the miracle of Bolsena.

As has happened so frequently in papal history, politics came into play and the grand church commemorating this miracle was constructed not in humble Bolsena, where the miracle had actually occurred, but in the grand city of Orvieto, twenty miles away—the biggest tourist hijacking in history. And so it came to pass that the famous city of Orvieto became even more renowned as the home of this stupendous cathedral, while little Bolsena went back to sleep on the shore of its lovely lake, seemingly unaware that it was once within a hand's grasp of immortality.

While Richard and I are walking through the streets, reflecting on this unusual tale, the clouds roll in and a bone-chilling wind blows in off the lake. This nasty turn in the weather casts a damper on the street market in progress, with disgruntled vendors grumbling at the poor customer turnout. Apart from the odd brave soul, the town is quite dead. For once, Bolsena seems a gloomy place. It gets gloomier still when Richard and I can't find a restaurant open for lunch. After a long and tetchy search, we eventually find a bar and settle on *panini*, which turn out to be stale and tasteless, proving that you really can get bad food in Italy. We stare at the dry *panini*, which look like the plastic food that might come with a toy kitchen play set. We eat them anyway, disgusted at ourselves, and leave the bar in a bad mood.

By chance, we come upon an open *trattoria*, tucked away down an alley, occupied by one lone customer. We remind ourselves that we have an iron-clad rule about only eating in restaurants that are full (based on the fact that Italians know their food and would rather wait for a table at a good restaurant than dine at an empty one), but we decide that today we will suspend the rule, and will also pretend that we never had lunch. The lone diner seems to be thoroughly enjoying himself, and is consumed with his lunch, a wonderful meat dish and a bottle of wine he has all to himself. We tell the Signora we'll have what he is having. She beams with pleasure, saying that is their best dish—Veal *Scallopini alla Griglia* (*recipe page 339)* with spinach and roast potatoes (*recipe page 343). Within sight and smell of a good recoup, our spirits rise. We decide on a bottle of hearty Rosso di Montalcino, and the gloomy day takes on a distinctly happier aspect as we settle back in anticipation. We are not disappointed. The meal arrives in less time than it took to get our *panini,* and it's excellent.

We set off for our appointment with Dr. Ricci, the attorney who had helped us with the closing. We feel we have the right man; at the closing table he spent hours sizing up Signora Morelli and, more important, he faced her down during one of her outbursts. There probably aren't many people in our area who can claim to have done that. The sun comes out again as we stroll to his office along a lovely tree-lined boulevard that leads down to the lake.

Dr. Ricci sees us into his studio, and we describe what has occurred. He immediately picks up the phone and calls Signora Morelli. In a few staccato sentences he makes his point, and then puts her on the speaker phone. Signora Morelli angrily blurts out a rebuttal, or maybe it's an excuse. He makes no reply. She makes another excuse. Still he makes no reply. She goes on at some length, but is hesitant now, evidently digging herself into a hole. Dr. Ricci never says a word. She talks herself to a standstill, and then, rather lamely, she promises that she and her family will not set foot on our property again.

Dr. Ricci permits himself a faint smile, leans back in his chair, and says confidently, "You will never hear from those people again!"

❧⚘

Signora Gaspari, on learning of all this, gently and quickly taps her eyes.

"Watch those people," she says.

We report back to Clateo.

"Well, this lawyer of yours, maybe he did a good job," he says grudgingly. "But what I'd like to know is, how much did he charge you?" His head tilted back, bracing himself for an argument on one of his pet topics, he awaits our response.

This time it's our turn to chuckle. "Nothing," we reply.

12

MOLTO LAVORO

Let not ambition mock their noble toil!
(Gray's Elegy*)*

Friday is a big shopping day; the streets, which are usually deserted at this time of year, come to life. A vegetable truck arrives with its "drive-by shopping." It has to be a very quick transaction, as the street in Lubriano is so narrow. The truck stops right outside my door, and I run out, asking for a kilo of *pomodori*—tomatoes. Mr. Umbrian Vegetables weighs them with lightening speed so that he will not hold up traffic. I wander down to the little *alimentari* and buy some *mozzarella di bufala* to make some wonderful fresh *Caprese* Salad. In Italy, if you ask for basil when you buy your tomatoes, they will throw it in free. Despite the fact that I have not bought the tomatoes at Luigina's Frutteria, she gives me the basil at no charge. She hands me a large bunch of basil; the roots are still attached. So I have the ingredients for *Caprese* Salad (*recipe page 277): fresh sliced tomatoes, fresh sliced mozzarella, and lots of basil, with some left to plant. The salad is drizzled with olive oil and lemon juice or vinegar, and then sprinkled with salt and pepper. It is just as simple as that.

A *Caprese* Salad can show you the difference between produce in Italy and produce in America. A *Caprese* in Italy tastes like a fresh spring morning, while a *Caprese* in America, made with supermarket tomatoes and over-processed mozzarella, can taste like a cardboard box.

Tonight I will serve my *Caprese* with my simple Herbed Chicken from the last cookbook I wrote *Cooking for My Friends*, which I published in 1998 (*recipe page 321).

It's now time to go in for the kill and try to round up some workmen to help us with a remodel. I have absolutely no idea how to start. One of the little cantinas down the street is being converted into a fine lingerie shop. Not exactly what you think of when Lubriano still doesn't have anything but the basics— two butchers, two little supermarkets, one vegetable and wine store, one restaurant, one pizzeria, and one bar/coffee/gelato shop, and here we have La Perla lingerie moving in? Perhaps this is a sign of what is in store for Lubriano. There is a man in there putting the finishing touches on the most meticulously laid *cotto* tile floor. He tells me that it is framed with "typical Umbrian-design tiles." I have stopped by to ask him if he does work around here. The young man looks more like a merchant banker than a tile layer. He is excited to meet me and tells me that his father has a big tile factory up the road, as well as a villa that he has just finished restoring. It's looking promising.

We then meet up with the newly found worker and his father and look at their tile factory. I have my suspicions that he won't want to undertake our work, as he looks awfully smart to be a laborer. But how do you know where to begin? It's amazing: when you dig a little deeper than a person just renting a house in the area, you find a whole system that you didn't know existed. There are no advertisements, so you have to have eyes like a hawk. I am completely underwhelmed by the factory's entrance, and yet behind it is a sophisticated building with a wonderful showroom of elegant bathrooms and kitchens. His father, Gregorio, welcomes us. He is a handsome man who tells us that he thinks some big American movie star has just bought a home near Orvieto. Gregorio appears to speak very good English, but when I try and talk to him I can clearly see that he doesn't really understand me. He says he will show us some of his work and please to follow him in our car. He will, he says, also send us a carpenter.

He takes us to look over his work at his house, which has a view similar to ours looking over Civita. It is not a restored house, but a beautifully constructed new villa. Their goals and sights are set on the new, and my sights are set on maintaining the integrity of a sixteenth-century building. I have a sneaking suspicion that after a couple of years of restoration we may think this would have been an excellent buy for us— particularly as my husband has a reputation for staying well clear of any project that doesn't include a pen and paper.

Gregorio confirms my suspicion that we may have been better off buying a new place when he tells me that the house his mother has been living in for sixty years (very close to our house) is in danger of falling down and needs a new roof. Also, all the beams holding the floors and ceilings are completely rotten and in danger of collapse; they will have to put iron stays in the outer walls to keep them upright.

It's just as well we never had a structural walk-through; we would never have bought Braccioforte.

Gregorio shows me the fireplace made of basalt, which looks like a dull, charcoal-gray granite. He says there is an ancient *basaltina* quarry a couple of kilometers away. It's an historical quarry used by the Romans to adorn much of Rome. In those times the Tiber River was navigable right up to our Calanchi Valley. Today the Tiber at this location is nothing more than a stream. He also says there is a man in Bagnoregio who works with this stone, so we will see where this path leads us. I think it will be good to use this *basaltina* in our house, as we have two *basaltina* fireplaces already. Some Jesuit monk must have picked this out, too, about five hundred and fifty years ago.

These people are most hospitable, but my suspicions are confirmed. In reality, they're not interested in helping us with our remodel. They would rather we (or one of our family members) buy their new villa. The son arrives at our house and wants us to throw out everything.

"Medieval is out and modern is in. Everything must go," he says.

The good news is, at least he showed up. The carpenter doesn't even show up. I hope that this is not a sign of the "on time" habits of local workmen, but I have an ominous suspicion that I am in for more of this tardiness.

Richard and I are a little dejected by our false start. We return to the *annesso* and, cathartically, try getting through to the depths of the ten-by-twenty-foot space. Considering the minute size of the rooms, Signora Morelli certainly could pack in a lot.

Today we uncover an iron bed base that had been completely covered by Mario's ubiquitous vine. We find some wonderful old windows and doors, heavy as lead; I have no idea why they were ever replaced in the first place.

Richard and I hack back some vegetation. The garden is beginning to present itself. We notice in the garden next to ours that Signora Morelli's cousin or some ancestor had made a lovely garden table by cutting down an apple or a pear tree to about table height and then balancing a very old stone, about three by four feet, (maybe from a Jesuit) on the three arms extending from the trunk. It's quite charming, but behind the unkempt garden it is almost impossible to see.

I am startled to see a bird that I thought was only found in South Africa in my Italian backyard. A comical hoopoe, the favorite bird of my children because of its rusty zebra-striped crest, hops out from behind a shrub as if to say, "Oh! Are you here too?" I had no idea these birds migrate all the way from Africa to charm the Italian springtime.

Spring has definitely sprung. *Primavera*. Our first daffodil is up this morning, with many more to follow, and all the birds are singing in the garden in Braccioforte.

Richard becomes friendly with the son of the owner of the nearby restaurant Trattoria del Pozzo. His name is Mauro. Mauro has taken on the duty of introducing Richard to all the bars and nightclubs in the area. We and our family, while renting the villa nearby, have eaten at Trattoria del Pozzo many times over the past years. Mauro suggests that we go to an old *non importante* furniture shop in the countryside on the way to Montefiascone and Viterbo. This store is filled with discards and some hidden treasures—if you can get past the sheep grazing between broken winepresses and the bank of four old joined-together hair salon chairs with hairdryers above that looks like a lunar landing vehicle for four astronauts.

The inside of the store is equally bizarre. A

ratty old stuffed fox, sitting on top of a vintage computer, gives you a wily look as you enter. Richard buys a very old writing table that looks so simple it is modern in its antiquity. He is a minimalist, content with a bed and a writing table, and living out of a suitcase is fine with him. I buy a huge old armoire ten feet long. The owner of the store says he will disassemble it and reassemble it in our bedroom. He says it is called a "Four Seasons" because it has room for clothes for the whole year. The prices are unbelievably low, and I am sure we will thank Mauro many times for bringing us here as we attempt to furnish Braccioforte.

This morning, right on the dot, the owner of the store arrives with the armoire I have bought yesterday. Deliveries are a problem with our nine-foot-wide streets. The truck stops hurriedly and the two men jump out to deliver the partially disassembled armoire before the next car comes along. As they take the armoire off the truck it suddenly looks really large. They struggle through the old arched gate and up the ten stairs to the front door. They have another struggle to get it into the bedroom, and then it suddenly shrinks. It looks dwarfed when set down. Everything is a matter of perspective. The room without furniture, which I had thought of as medium-size, suddenly becomes a large medieval room. I am happy; this is a start, this beautiful, high-ceilinged room.

No delivery charge, he says.

It's a start.

I drive to the terracotta factory opposite Casteluzzo, the farmhouse we have rented many times. They have some wonderful terracotta tables. The old guard dog is sitting outside the factory trying to get anyone to let him back in. It's interesting to see Casteluzzo peacefully sitting in the distance, as we are looking at it from the opposite direction; we used to look across the road at the little terracotta factory grinding the clay and turning it into precious objects.

Samantha, who works at the terracotta factory, says, "I believe there is a wonderful *piscina* (pool) there!"

I nod for, blessedly, I know this very well. Yes, and it brought us to this place.

I am determined to get started with some of our remodel. In the meantime, we take the path of least resistance, and Gloria's husband Mario goes beyond being our self-appointed handyman and gardener to become our self-appointed *muratore*. He is now Mario the Builder. He arrives with two friends, and the three of them standing there together look as though they have just stepped out of a movie on doing remodels in Italy—Mario, wild and fiery; then tall, thin Andrea with a very large nose and completely covered from head to toe in dust; and Agostino, Andrea's father, about half the size of Andrea, with a little, wrinkled, timeworn face like a monkey and an impish, naughty grin. He wears a very grubby disposable painter's hat perched on the back of his head. More importantly, they have tools with them and are ready for the word "go" to begin with whatever we want.

Andrea and Mario are experienced workers, but Dad Agostino seems to go at things like a bull at a gate. He is definitely part of the bash-down crew. Ancient pieces of plaster go flying all over our kitchen. Despite his minute size, he has immense strength, and the two young men keep on sending him down the road for more bags of cement. He flings them with ease over his shoulder and, cigarette in mouth, he skips up the stairs as though carrying a feather pillow.

Mario does all the remodeling in the Palazzo and is also their general handyman, which makes me a little more confident. He has been trained to take a rustic medieval wall and make it look perfect like an American wall, and despite my many protestations that the wall is smooth enough they continue to try to make it smoother—virtually impossible with a five-hundred-year-old structure, especially with its odd angles and impossible non-squares.

I have been trying to put into words all week, without offending them, that they're doing far too good a job. I eventually have an idea and stand in front of a crack that looks similar to the one that an artist had faux painted on our kitchen wall in Denver. At that moment Mario and Andrea are trying desperately to smooth over honest-to-goodness, real live cracks.

"Look," I say, "people are paying huge amounts of money in Beverly Hills to make their walls look just like this cracked wall, and here you are getting stomach ulcers trying to make this wall smooth and refined, whereas I am very happy with these cracks." (Gloria is translating.)

They look at me, aghast.

"But we are fine workmen! We cannot leave a wall like this—what will your husband think when he comes into town and sees this wall?"

"Trust me!" I tell them through Gloria, "My husband is happy with any wall, particularly if he doesn't have to be involved with it."

"He is a smart person!" says Gloria.

I try to think of a way to make them appreciate that *rustica* is fine. I tell them that there are many movie stars who have people come into their houses and, with the aid of all sorts of devices, make their work look rough and rustic. They're not very convinced. They try hard to do a bad job, but I can see that it's painful for them. At last they finish restoring all the plasterwork, and after I offer them a couple of beers, they're somewhat mollified.

Gloria has been cleaning up after Mario, Andrea, and Agostino, who seem to think that carting off piles of rubble is women's work. She is really more interested in being our Yellow Pages and foreman. She does not like cleaning, nor is she very good at it. The minute Gloria has all the mess out of the way, the men begin making a mess again. We could go on like this indefinitely, for sure. Gloria is constantly bossing them around, but they don't listen. She shouts out, "Mario makes the mess, Gloria cleans!"

She says to me in an aside that she is *Carabinieri* (Police) Gloria and that she has to watch them all the time so they don't make mistakes. Richard and I find ourselves in a residence that is about two inches deep in paint and plaster dust. David, luckily for him, is in the USA, getting ready to wind down his career. It's hard to get into bed with such a mess, so we begin to mop. After two hours each night, however, we are exhausted and still can't see the terracotta floors for all the mess. We just call it a day. After all, this is Italy.

13

IL POZZO – THE WELL

Mr. Mario, tear down this wall!
(Apologies to Ronald Reagan)

Today has been set aside to paint the kitchen. The kitchen has a big heart, and we will start with the heart of the home. It's a tedious job, to be sure, but we need to get it done to make the house livable. Richard and I are up early. A quick cup of coffee and we get to work, preparing the materials and starting the task of scraping layers of paint from the walls. We little realize that, before the day is done, painting walls will no longer be on our agenda, and that another "project" will have pulled us away from our intended labors.

We have engaged Andrea, who has worked for us before and is reputed to be an expert on the painting of these old *tufa* walls. Andrea has promised to arrive by 9 a.m., and Mario will be here to assist with the work. Richard and I are ready, willing, and able to pitch in and help, so we are looking forward to a day of significant progress.

Around 10 a.m. we realize that our plans are probably going to be frustrated again, as none of our helpers have arrived. After a few more cups of coffee, Gloria appears, and assures us that Mario is on the way. A short while later Mario arrives with their two children, but he has left their faithful dog Tiny at home. Gloria is annoyed, Mario defensive.

After a brief verbal scuffle between the two of them, it is decided that the family cannot start work while Tiny is penned up in their apartment, so Mario is sent home to retrieve him. When he returns, Tiny entertains us by racing around the garden with a pinecone in his mouth, one ear up and one down. "A truffle hound, Signora," Gloria asserts confidently. "A very special dog. Very special!"

We look at him with some doubt, thinking that he looks a bit like a gone-wrong dachshund, and we hope that he will lose interest in his pinecone soon so that the day's work can commence.

After a final cup of coffee, we give up on Andrea and decide to get started. Richard, Mario, and I get out our scrapers and go to work on the kitchen walls. Mario is a fierce worker, with huge strength and energy, but in spite of our exertions we soon realize that this is going to be a tougher undertaking than we had bargained for. We scrape and scrape, but seem to make very little progress on these often-painted walls. Layers and layers of dusty lime wash, powdery whitewash, and gritty who-knows-what-wash come falling down on us until we look like powdery white ghosts. To make matters worse, in our efforts to remove generations of paint, we start to dislodge big chunks of plaster, exposing the bare rock behind them. How, we wonder, can we paint these walls if the very walls themselves are falling around us?

Ankle-deep in dust and rubble, we are starting to feel despondent, when the door opens and Andrea appears. I think again that he looks uncannily like the Man of La Mancha. His tall, skinny frame and beak-like Etruscan nose complete the picture. Quite unfazed by the chaotic scene around him, he pulls out his scraper and launches a vigorous assault on the walls. More dust, dirt, and plaster come falling down, until I am afraid that instead of restoring the house we are wrecking it. Shoulder-to-shoulder with Andrea, Mario is also hammering at the walls, scraping, scraping.

Mario is turning out to be an amazing workman. I don't think he can read very well, for I see him getting Gloria to read instructions to him. His mind, however, is as sharp as six tacks.

Suddenly, in the middle of an energetic pounding with his scraper, Mario stops. He holds up his hand, cocks his head, and seems to be listening to something. "*Silenzio!*"

He raises his fist and pounds on the wall in front of him, listens carefully and pounds again. This time I can hear it too. The wall gives off a distinctly hollow sound.

"*Allora!* Signora," he says flatly.

He stands back and puts his hands on his hips, shaking his head. I look at him anxiously. What does this mean? Have we discovered yet another problem, a collapsing wall in the heart of our house? To my consternation, he grabs a crowbar and bashes a brick out of the wall!

"*Strano!*"—Strange! he yells. Catching his excitement, I take the crowbar and start pounding on the wall too. The bricks give way, and a hole appears at eye level. A whoosh of cold air hits me in the face as the air escapes. We pull out more bricks and shine a flashlight into the gloom.

Through the swirling dust, we are astonished to find ourselves looking into the depths of an ancient well. Bricked up, sealed off, its existence completely forgotten, it is for us a magical discovery in our journey into the history of our house. Standing there looking into the dusty depths of the well, we can't help wondering what other ancient secrets it has to show us.

Mario votes for removing the rest of the wall.

"This wall is so thin, I will break it with my hands," he says with a swagger.

And so he does. He breaks pieces of masonry as though he were cracking nuts. Through the larger opening we can now discern the well walls, and, above the well itself, some ancient beams from a long-forgotten staircase leading to who knows where. A rotten old rope hangs from a rusted spindle in front of our faces.

We gather around the opening in the wall to discuss this exciting find. The top of the well is about three feet wide, but as it descends it widens abruptly to about fifteen feet. The bottom is at least twenty-five feet below us, covered with a layer of rubble, and my heart beats faster at the thought of excavating this ancient trove. Richard is as excited as I am at this prospect. Gloria, as usual, takes it all in stride, as though she discovers ancient wells every day.

"Oh, yes, Signora, an old well. It probably got used as a trash dump when the water gave out. Excavate it? Why do you want to do that, Signora? Nothing important in there, believe me. No treasures in Lubriano, Signora. Everyone in Lubriano has always been poor. Nothing worth finding in there! Believe me."

But we don't believe her. We think this old well may tell us more about our house than we have yet learned, and we look forward excitedly to the time when we can uncover its secrets.

છ∾✧

It is Sunday, the day after our discovery of the well. For once, we are hoping for a late start to the day, and assume that, as usual, our workers will show up hours late, or probably not at all. Once again, our expectations are confounded when our doorbell rings insistently at 8 a.m. Reluctantly, we open the gate to let our workers in, only to discover that they have brought with them an enormous quantity of equipment to start the excavation of the well.

Word of our well discovery has spread around the town, and a buzz of excitement surrounds us. Our neighbor, Signora Gaspari, who knows everything about everything in Lubriano, is astonished. How could she have lived all her life just a few meters from this wonder and never dreamed of its existence?

"Ah, Signora, you have a *pozzo*—a well. *Brava, brava!*"

Other neighbors stop by to congratulate us. "*Complimenti, complimenti!*" we hear again and again—Congratulations, congratulations!

We take advantage of their interest to ask for opinions as to what we should do with this find. A small number agree that it would be exciting to excavate the well, but to our astonishment, many of them feel that the best idea is to cement it over! Oh, and it would be a good place to store our wine. We try to understand this attitude of enthusiasm mixed with indifference on the part of our neighbors, and arrive at the conclusion that Italy is so blessed with antiquities that people have become complacent, even blasé, about their heritage, and don't think it worth the effort to preserve it.

I receive a more gratifying reaction from my ten-year-old grandson in America. "Are you going to be famous, Di?" he asks. "Are you going to be in *National Geographic?*"

In any case, it's our well, and we have decided what we are going to do—we are going to carefully excavate it in the hope that we will unearth something of value, historical or otherwise. At the very least, we hope to learn something of the history of the house. We have heard some stories of reopening ancient wells, thanks to friends who have spent time in Italian villas. The most attention-getting was the story of a well in nearby Cortona. When the new owners of a villa discovered that it contained an ancient well, they excitedly started to excavate it. Their first horrifying discovery was that it contained the bodies of German soldiers from World War II, I suppose simply dumped there after some terrible but long-forgotten battle. They emptied earth and then cement down the well and left the dead in peace. So I tell our workers that I am hoping for no dead people from the past in my well—no Germans, no Partisans, no Romans, no Etruscans!

Andrea takes charge of the excavations. As usual, his cigarette dangles precariously from his lip. His eyes are like slits against the ambient smoke, making him look as though he is permanently walking into the wind. The excavation equipment is unloaded and brought into the house. The centerpiece is an old, electric-powered winch that looks as though it should have been retired many years ago. Then there is a long ladder and a number of poles that are supposed to fit into each other and create some kind of scaffolding structure. After a long period of trying to fit the poles together, accompanied by some contentious exchanges between Mario and Andrea, it is decided that we should dispense with the poles and rely on the winch and the ladder.

In short order, these pieces of equipment are installed, and Andrea and Mario disappear down the ladder to get to work. Muffled conversations and arguments are heard from the depths of the well, but at length the sounds of shovels being applied takes over and we feel that progress is being made.

We have agreed that we will winch up buckets of rubble and sort them on the surface to see if we have found anything of importance. It soon becomes apparent that our workers have a somewhat different take on the objective than we do. The sounds of their shovels being lustily applied make us realize that they are intent on clearing everything out of the well, and the sooner the better. They're not slowed down by the thought of finding a Roman urn or a precious Etruscan artifact. Any such ambitions have clearly been shoveled aside, as copious quantities of dirt, rubble, fragments of pottery, and pieces of broken tiles are being hauled up by the winch.

Uneasily, I recall the story of Loretta, another Italian neighbor, who hired some workmen to dig up an old floor in a room in her house. When she checked back later, there lay a cup from Roman times, broken in two by a blow from a shovel. Sadly, it had lain unbroken for perhaps two thousand years, only to be destroyed in the few minutes that she had been away.

Chapter 13

In an attempt to avoid a similar disaster, I call a break in the work after a couple of hours, so we can take stock of what we have found. It's time to stop the shovels being speared into the dirt before some *objet d'art* is shattered by a forceful blow from Mario. The workers, having hit their stride, are in no mood to stop, so I call down that there is fresh coffee brewing. At this, Andrea scrambles up the ladder with astonishing agility. Considering that the ladder is twenty-five feet down, at an almost vertical angle, not to mention that it has several missing rungs and a few more that look ready to go, this looks like a dangerous operation, but at least I have got him out of the well. He steps into the kitchen, picks up two cups of coffee, balances himself precariously on top of the ladder, and proceeds to walk down it, with his back to the rungs, his hands clutching the coffee cups and his ever-present cigarette dangling from his lips.

After a few minutes the digging sounds start again. With some chagrin, I realize that although I often can't get these two to work when I want them to work, now I can't get them to stop when I want them to stop.

Finally lunch time arrives, the digging stops, and we all gather round the pile of dirt that Richard and I have hauled out into the garden. To be candid, it's a somewhat dispiriting sight. Our treasure trove consists mainly of builders' rubble, chunks of concrete, and other rubbish of a decidedly twentieth-century provenance.

But buried in this mound of rubbish I find a few slivers of broken pottery, and suddenly I get the feeling that down in this long-lost well we may yet find something to treasure.

Our diggers are distinctly uninterested in our finds. They're in the camp that favors the cementing-over-and-storing-wine-down-there solution. We point out that it makes no sense to store our wine in a place that is going to require a twenty-five-foot climb down a perilous vertical ladder when we can easily store it in the kitchen, but they're unmoved.

Lunch is over and the digging starts again. More rubble comes up, and then the scene changes. In a few moments, we realize we have dug below World War II levels. No dead Germans, no bodies of any type (thank goodness), but we are past the rubble and into an earlier era. Hidden in the dry, sandy dirt, we gradually start to find pieces of long-ago broken pottery with lovely rustic designs, maybe a hundred or even two hundred years old. An hour later we are a hundred years earlier than that. And then one piece of ceramic ware is sifted out of the pile of dirt: a small, broken piece of an ancient plate, decorated with hand-painted concentric circles in deep blue, aqua and yellow. This is a find. Simply by looking at it you can tell that it's something very old, something wonderful.

"*Basta!*" I shout to Mario and Andrea. Enough! Stop. Stop now.

We are done for the day. I'm afraid that if they keep going, any similar pieces of pottery will be smashed by their over-enthusiastic shovels. It has been a good day, and they're ready to stop. Disdaining even the marginal safety of the rickety ladder, they haul themselves up via the even more marginal safety of the ancient winch. We settle down in the kitchen and open a bottle of wine to celebrate. Gloria, so often our life-saver appears with an enormous just-made *Tiramisu* (*recipe page 351). She would have made it this morning, she says, but she was waiting for the egg-man to arrive with today's eggs. Make a *tiramisu* with yesterday's eggs? She bursts out laughing at the very thought of such foolishness.

We open another bottle of wine and work our way through most of the *Tiramisu*. Tiny the Dog looks at us pleadingly until we give him a spoonful.

"Just one!" says Gloria. "Otherwise he won't sleep!"

Tiny gobbles his portion and goes in search of his pinecone. He, too, has had a good day.

I'll take our precious find to an expert in Orvieto, and we will learn something more about the age of our well and the age of our house. I explain this to Andrea and Mario. They look dubious. I can see what they're thinking. Why get excited about bits of old pottery? Why not do what any sensible Italian would do with this well—dig out the loose rubble, cement over the debris, and keep your wine down there?

When next in Orvieto I decide to go into one of the many ceramic shops and ask about our little piece of pottery from the *pozzo*. I find a shop that looks as though it has more ancient designs than the normal

Tuscan blend of flowers and fruits. The owner fingers my piece of broken pottery and looks interested. He brings out his book on medieval ceramics and within about two minutes has opened it to a page with an exact copy of our piece of pottery—the same colors and concentric circles in golden, blue, and turquoise. It is fifteenth-century, he says. He says that if we found this pottery right at the top of the *pozzo*, who knows what is underneath?

14

BOUNTY HUNTERS

Gloria arrives, insisting that we have her lasagna for lunch; we protest that she doesn't have to feed us, but she says she would be offended if we didn't accept. Again it's packed full of flavor. She makes lasagna with a béchamel sauce and layers and layers filled with porcini mushrooms and sausage, then bakes it in the oven with a thick layer of Parmesan cheese on top (*recipe page 305).

Richard says, "We are trying to pay these people wages, but they're giving us back all the wages in food and extracurricular time." And this is to say nothing of their many kindnesses.

Tomorrow Mario is bringing a gardener to work for us, and is coming himself with Andrea. They have already constructed the scaffold in the *salone* (room with a fresco) and will get to work tomorrow on unfolding more secrets.

One step at a time.

Today we have to go to the *Comune*—City Hall—because the glass is broken on the water meter. I gather we are responsible for fixing it. Richard's Italian is progressing at a phenomenal pace. I am literally being left in the dust. He walks to the *Comune*, which is about a quarter of a mile from town. The man attending to him tells him that they will have to hurry with the transaction, as he has to drive the school bus. Richard is a little puzzled when the official insists on his getting in the school bus. Hurry, hurry, he says—the schoolchildren are waiting. He speeds off, or attempts to speed off. He jolts the school bus to a halt right outside the tiny little hardware store, hazard lights flashing, leads Richard quickly inside, grabs a water meter off a shelf, and shoves it into Richard's hands. He smiles and waves, and the school bus disappears in the dust.

Mario and Andrea are back, working a mile a minute. Mario is ripping electrical cord out of the wall and putting in new wiring, all without turning off the main electrical box. They make us in the USA all look like sissies.

Andrea all of a sudden hops onto the entrance to the well and asks Mario to let him down into its depths: they didn't have the ladder again today. So, cringing, I watch as Mario slowly, via the skimpy winch, lets Andrea down the twenty feet. I wonder what on earth he needs to be doing at the bottom of the well. It turns out he has left his cigarettes there two days ago.

The day is beautiful, with a blue Colorado-type sky, and the daffodils are out in earnest. The apple trees are in blossom in the garden in front of us. They add to the already spectacular view of Civita. In the evening glow at twilight, they look luminously white, with the whole outcrop of the town of Civita silhouetted behind the tree and Civita itself silhouetted in front of the deep-pink late evening sky.

The local garden expert who has been sent around by Mario to look at our garden is here. This property, he says, probably has not had any attention in about twenty years. He looks like the gardener from *Desperate Housewives*—impossibly good-looking, as so many young Italian men are. He notes that we have infestations of *processionario* worms, whatever those may be, in our Roman pines. I shrug this off immediately. I'll save this problem for another day. I have more problems to solve than mere worms. As Finnish people say, "I will put this behind my ear," along with Signora Gaspari's root problem.

The gardener spends a good long while trying to work out how he can get a Rototiller up our steep entry stairs and through our large iron gates. In medieval times back entrances were a bad security idea, so there is none to our garden. I did suggest we use Andrea's winch to hoist the equipment from the farmer's field down below, but that suggestion does not fly.

Richard and I drive towards Orvieto today. We are in desperate search of a carpenter, and are coming up blank on our carpenter search. It's a beautiful drive. At the moment, all the fallow fields are filled with rye grass and everything is a bright green. The "No Bush/USA" graffiti is a little unsettling, particularly as we are driving by serenely grazing sheep. We drive through the beautiful hamlet of Canale and all of a sudden see a sign indicating a carpenter's workshop. We screech to a halt and follow scattered signs over an indistinct track through a pasture and past a couple of cows, around the side of an ancient farmhouse, and eventually to a sign saying *Bottega Falegnameria*—Carpenter's Workshop—hoping that this man lives far away enough from Lubriano not to know that he shouldn't show up. Our kitchen is still a blank slate with a faucet sticking out of the wall.

The carpenter follows us home and comes up with a bid on the spot, shocking us into complete silence. We were expecting to receive the quote some weeks later, or, more likely, never.

Signora Gaspari extends her head out of the door at the sight of an out-of-towner walking into our house. As the carpenter leaves, she greets me again with more *"Radice, radice."* I reply again with a *"Non capisco,"* shrugging my shoulders, trying to buy myself another few days before addressing the root problem.

I take Signora Gaspari into our kitchen to show her the new state of the *pozzo*—a political move to subtly show her we are busy with other things. She also suggests the old "cement-over-the-*pozzo*" trick. After all, there is only all that old broken junk down there. I have a hard time understanding her, and I complain to Gloria that I just cannot understand Signora Gaspari. Gloria, for once, tries to act the diplomat: she tells me that it is Signora Gaspari's Lubrianese/Italian dialect and not my patchy Italian.

Signor Gaspari wanders in with a slightly disapproving look on his face, startled by our "restoration" in the kitchen. In his opinion, we are going backwards. He sees that we had exposed some of the ancient *tufa* by removing the plaster. He looks a little suspicious about this *tufa* showing through, as exposed *tufa* is considered peasant-like. The Lubriano Town Council, in fact, has decreed that no house front should have bare stone and should be plastered. Plastering or cementing over the past seems to be a thing around here. We should apparently ignore the fact that the house was plaster-free for six hundred years. Perhaps some plain white paint would suit the Signor's taste. If he had his way, he would whip those workmen into shape. Everything on his beat would be crackless, starched, and sterile, hospital-style. He is very earnest and very polite, and I don't think he could ever get the whole Tuscany craze thing in the USA at all.

In contrast, Gloria sits down with me this afternoon to discuss whether our fresco was before or after Imperial. "It is definitely before Baroque," she tells me. She backs this up with a comment that she spent a year training in art. She also has a year's training in physical therapy and enough of a smattering of other types of "training" that you should not argue with her. With all this "training," she should be a hundred and not thirty-six. She says there is a style between Imperial and Baroque; perhaps it fits into that school. She tells me there is a restorer working on frescoes in the Palazzo; she will send him over to have a look at our lady who gazes sweetly down at us with a wire cord gouged into her belly.

15

IL SUONO DELLA MUSICA –
THE SOUND OF MUSIC

*Whenever a friend succeeds, a little something in me
dies!
(Gore Vidal)*

I bump into Angelo Giordano in the bank this morning. He is the owner of the Palazzo, but certainly doesn't look like a lord of the manor with his stubble and his worn jeans. He looks more like a happy and contented version of Mussolini. He and his wife have eight children, all living in the palace, ranging in age from twenty-three to eight years old. He invites us to come and look at the private rooms in his palace. This is quite a grand gesture, I gather, particularly as Richard and I are currently covered from head to toe with construction dust. We are looking rather like vagabonds.

"*Brava*, Deeaaanahh! *Vieni*," says Angelo, shaking my hand so furiously and beaming so widely that I could see he was looking through all the dust. His English is poor, but he compensates by inserting "Deeaaanahh" in between every second word with such sincerity that we feel extraordinarily welcome.

Our dusty clothes look even dustier as we enter the palace proper. The main reception area is completely filled, wall-to-wall, with fifteen-foot-high paintings, which Angelo says he brought from his palace in Basilicata. Angelo shepherds us to the next room as Richard and I follow, hoping we don't run into anyone else.

The grand reception room boasts crystal chandeliers the size of small cars and elaborate paneling. It is apparently rented out for weddings. The grounds look like they are in need of a good watering and don't match the grandeur of such an interior. The gardens could be beautifully landscaped—and probably were, as there are marble staircases, large urns and statues dotting the property. There are fountains begging to be restarted and marble columns lying sleeping on the ground. Angelo also shows us three other reception rooms filled with Renaissance art and Belgian tapestries. He will invite us to dinner in the private palace rooms later, he tells us.

Gloria says that the family tries to keep the

opulence of the private rooms in the palace a secret from the town people. Of course, this is the world according to Gloria. The palace itself is less than imposing from the outside, so if this is their intent, they're doing a pretty good job. Some years ago someone obviously decided that the palace should be painted. *L' imbiancho*—the painter—had obviously tried out six different color swatches right next to their baronial front door. The weathered, forgotten color swatches, each two feet square, still remain; the palace goes unpainted, giving credence to Gloria's remark. It is a shabby cover on a richly illustrated book.

The great big old palace doors are worn and peeling. Mario parks his old Vespa scooter with a torn leather seat not twenty feet from the entrance. Ring the bell and someone will release a latch on the gray, peeling, sun-bleached wooden doors, which are big enough to ride a horse through. Entering, you find yourself in a partially covered cobbled courtyard. *Tanti anni fa*—many long years ago—riders dismounted here. The palace proper begins at the top of a flight of stairs that lead directly off this courtyard. The three apartments that the Giordanos rent out to tourists also lead off from the courtyard at this ancient entrance. All in all, given the facade and the general outside appearance of the public quarters, they're doing a pretty good job of fooling people into judging a book by its cover. The palace, Angelo says, was also part of a monastery, and in the fifteenth century it was converted into a hunting lodge.

Angelo's late father bought the place about

fifteen years ago. He and his son began restoring it and embellished the property significantly. They added many frescoes to match the existing ones and have filled the palace with fine works of art. White marble busts of Roman senators, beautiful tapestries, and fine Renaissance paintings fill every salon and hall.

Gloria, adding to the drama, says they found an Etruscan tomb here and quickly covered it up with the old "cement-over" trick so as not to have their entire courtyard roped off by some overzealous government archaeologist.

Gloria is a never-ending source of "upstairs/downstairs" chatter. She has an amusing story that sends me into a fit of giggles. Apparently Signora Giordano once entertained some Japanese guests and used Gloria as a translator. She speaks perfect Italian, Spanish, Tagalog and English; therefore, Signor Giordano somehow assumed she could speak Japanese too.

Signor Giordano beckoned Gloria to stand between him and the Japanese guests and demanded, "Ask them what they like to eat."

"But I don't speak Japanese, Signore!"

"Well, ask them anyway!"

Gloria does a wonderful mime, ham that she is. "The Japanese reply, 'Aaah... *Si*!'" says Gloria (she hadn't understood a word they'd said).

She told the Signore, "They like raw fish and raw everything else. They don't like anything cooked too much."

With this ill-gotten knowledge, Angelo's wife prepares the meal. A whole raw fish from the local fish truck is washed under some tepid water and slapped on the dinner table. I am sure that there is no such thing as a "sushi quality" designation from the fish-on-wheels cart.

"She took me literally when cooking the pasta too," says Gloria, "She cooked the pasta by barely passing it through hot water. It was what I would like to call *Spaghetti a la Militari*, as each strand of pasta was standing there at attention on the plate."

Gloria does begrudgingly throw in an aside: "Normally, Signora Carmela is a very good cook."

16

ITALIAN NEIGHBORS

Good fences make good neighbors!
(English proverb)

Today we cross a barrier with the neighbors. Signora Gaspari tells us that we should now call them "Pasquina and Rinaldo" rather than Signore and Signora Gaspari. I think Pasquina has realized that we will probably be good neighbors. *Anything is better than Signora Morelli*, I think. This change to informal grammar is going to be difficult, as it severely affects my rudimentary Italian. I don't know how to change from the formal *lei*—you to the informal *tu*—you. A whole new set of rules apply that simply don't exist in English.

As we part, Pasquina rushes into the house and comes out with a little platter of chicken, which appears to have been simmered with many olives, sage, and white wine. I take a taste. It's really fabulous. When I compliment her, Rinaldo gives a shrug and looks bored—he has probably eaten this every Monday night for the past fifty years.

Signora Gaspari comes back into our little shared courtyard with a light bulb in hand and points to the lovely iron lamp at the top of our communal stairs. It's right outside our main gate and only seems to be activated from outside the Gaspari's door, though our doors are just fifteen feet apart. I feel bad to think that they might be paying for this common entrance light. Pasquina then points out to Richard that the light has a place for two bulbs and not one. This is a very clever system where, in the same light fixture, both the Gasparis and the Armstrongs can switch on the light from outside their front door. We are not surprised to learn that when Signora Morelli left she took her light bulb out of this fixture along with everything else.

The apartment above us is owned by the Morelli cousins. It is a two-storey affair, and it appears that the top floor is abandoned. I make inquiries today about whether the cousins would be interested in selling. One cousin lives in Rome and the other in Basilicata. If we are going to buy it and thereby have the whole *palazzino*, we would want to do so quite quickly before improving our property too much, which would add considerable value to their abandoned property. It looks as though it's been a good twenty-five years since it has been inhabited. We will see. If we bought it, the property might become another "be careful what you wish for" adventure.

I keep in mind our friend Peter's advice on Italian neighbors. I think we need to look after the relationships with the neighbors that we DO have. I remember Peter saying that sharing a meal together is terribly important to Italians, and that the finest thing we could do would be to invite our *vicini di casa* to break bread with us. I'm sure Signora Gaspari—sorry, Pasquina—will look at our food as though it was brought down from the moon. Nothing cooked in Lubriano seems to vary from the ancient ways. This is borne out by Rinaldo's turning up his nose at his wife's succulent Chicken with Olives.

In the name of good neighborliness we invite some of the neighbors to come for dinner too and enjoy our back garden (twenty-five people in all). Giuseppina in the butcher shop insists that I buy a whole loin of pork weighing about six pounds. She very carefully slits the meat away from the bone (a procedure called "chining") so that the meat is almost entirely separated from the bone but remains attached to it at the very tip of the chop. With instructions from her and four other ladies who stand waiting in the butcher shop, I lay four large sprigs of sage in the slit and about one pound of sausage meat mixed with some chopped scallions on top of it and skewer the whole lot together, placing it in a baking pan in the oven at a very high heat to seal the deal. I surround the roast with celery and olives and pour some olive oil and white wine over the meat, letting it cook for three hours until the wine has completely evaporated and the roast has turned a crispy brown. I serve this with a pasta from our area called *Pappardelle con Funghi* (*recipe page 295), which has been suggested by Luigina at the fruit and vegetable shop. She and yet more locals coach me to cook the pasta with a mix of the local mushrooms, including porcini, sizzled with some pancetta, olive oil, butter, and sage. All this is cooked at high heat until crisp, then tossed into the pasta. Everyone loves it, sitting there in our walled garden surrounded by cherry, olive, and fig trees. We all sit in a large circle, the odd person wandering to the back of the garden to pick a fig.

Cecily and Clateo are here too. She comes with a lovely gift. She brings, unannounced, a fabulous Pavlova (*recipe page 353), cooked but not assembled, to be put together just at the right time before eating. In the warmth of the evening the cream just won't whip, so she asks me for some sugar to help hasten the process. I reach for the sugar container and scoop into the cream a good tablespoon's worth. Dinner is served, and Giuseppina's pork is a wonderful success, as is the Pasta with Funghi.

I have also prepared a long-time favorite salad of mine from Tuscany called *Panzanella*, or Tuscan Bread Salad (*recipe page 279). It is perfect for a large group, as it can be made well in advance. In the prime of summer, overripe tomatoes can also be used, making it a perfect "leftover" dish for stale bread and slightly soft tomatoes.

Also, in anticipation of much hosting, I have prepared a week in advance a large quantity of my own homemade Italian *gelato* (*recipe page 349). I scoop it onto plates to serve along with the gift of the Pavlova. Everyone has been highly effusive about Giuseppina's pork and Luigina's mushroom pasta and the *Panzanella*, and yet an eerie silence settles over the group as everyone nurses their dessert.

Being a good hostess, I serve myself last, and spoon a slice of the Pavlova into my mouth. Horror of horrors, that sugar I gave Cecily to put in her dessert was actually salt.

Everyone had very politely been going into the kitchen and shoveling their dessert into the garbage bin, much to the consternation of the kitchen help. Just imagine what my gaffe did for the reputation of American cooks.

Someone actually had said, "The *gelato* is great!" but I hadn't picked up on hint that the Pavlova was emphatically not.

I have no clue how salt got into my sugar container. The ceramic container clearly has the word "sugar" written on the top. But this time, the laughs were definitely on me!

17

AN AUTHORIZED HUNTER

And lo! The hunter of the East has caught
The Palace tower in a noose of light!
(Omar Khayyam)

We now turn our attention to the big Roman pines in the garden that have some nasty-looking things hanging on the branches, which we have been putting off thinking about. They look like white spiders' nests, about the size of a large apple. It is time to address this problem raised by our gardener. Gloria says that they definitely are *processionarios*.

And then we see them on the lawn. Here are brown hairy caterpillars, each an inch long, marching in a long line or procession, forming a strand about fifteen feet long.

"We had better be careful of them," Gloria says.

These caterpillars look as if they are doing a conga as they march across my pathway towards the kitchen. Another procession marches up the wall of Braccioforte, perfectly camouflaged and looking like a giant crack in the *tufa* stone wall.

Gloria says to be careful, as some people are madly allergic to them. Tiny, her little dog, is having another dizzy fit with his newfound freedom in our backyard. Suddenly he appears, whimpering, at our back door. His dachshund's pointed snout now appears as puffy as a parrotfish. Tiny is lucky to be in the presence of a couple of real animal lovers; Richard, with his soft heart and great presence of mind, runs off down the road to the *Farmacia*.

Italians are not known for their kindness to animals. The pharmacist probably doesn't dose dogs very often. Surprisingly, he very solemnly prescribes an antihistamine with the correct dosage to help a little mutt of a truffle dog overcome the worms' toxins. In no time at all, Tiny has his questionable looks back.

Our neighbor Vincenzo Rossi, who is a government official in Rome, arrives on my doorstep. His family is from Lubriano and he weekends here with his French-born artist wife. Ella came to Rome in the sixties and fell in love with Rome and Vincenzo. Vincenzo is a self-appointed aficionado in the town and not to be messed with. He is a small man with a

Harley bike and a personality to match. He has his thumb in a cast. He says he broke it pounding on the desk in Rome. He tells me that all the neighbors have been complaining about the *processionario* worms in the Morelli pine trees for many years, and yet, not surprisingly, Signora Morelli refused to do anything about them. She completely ignored about ten citations from the Lubriano Town Council. She refused to do anything about them as her late husband had been a big judge in Viterbo and she was not taking any nonsense from a mere City Hall of a small *villagio*. Vincenzo said that City Hall had kindly given us time to settle in before citing us for being the owners of these pests.

I agree right away, after the Tiny incident, that the *processionarios* have to be dealt with. He says the only solution is for hunters to come over and shoot their guns into our trees. This is not exactly the solution I had in mind. He says he will look for some hunters to come over tomorrow to shoot into our trees. He will also arrange for all the necessary permits on our behalf. He will contact the Forestry Service, because these trees are protected, and also go and talk to the *Comune* – City Hall. He is being kind, but his front door is also in the shadow of our tree. I do hope they call before they start shooting.

At night you can hear the worms falling out of the nest onto the lawn. This is not conducive to star gazing. Gloria insists that if they fall on you, you will land up in the hospital in Orvieto. Judging by the horror stories that come out of Orvieto Hospital, this is not something you want to risk doing, *processionarios* or not.

At about eight o'clock one misty, chilly, sleep-in Saturday morning, Vincenzo comes to our front door with an exceptionally well-clad hunter, armed and dangerous.

"Stay inside," he says. *"Pericoloso!"*

The hunter happens to be Federico, the son of the owner of the restaurant Trattoria del Pozzo, where we have eaten on many occasions. Federico is about twenty-two and stunningly handsome, with movie-star looks. He is big and tall and shy—not like any of the locals. He stands back on one foot and smiles diffidently, as though he would rather be sitting on a fence on some ranch in Colorado. He has on a full hunter's kit and looks as though he got lost on his way to a ritzy deer hunt.

Vincenzo pushes past Federico. "I have permission from the Forest Service and the *Comune* and the *carabinieri*—state police—and the *vigili*—municipal police—and we have their permission to start shooting," he says, shaking his early morning cigarette in my face.

One would think that World War III was about to commence. These are important worms.

"I will go and knock on windows and doors to inform all the neighbors that we are going to be shooting and please to stay inside."

I honestly doubt that anyone has gotten out of bed yet.

Bam! Bam! Bam!

Federico shoots into all the *processionario* nests in the trees. These nests of spun silk. They don't LOOK toxic. Nevertheless, about thirty shotgun blasts rock the town and all who are sleeping in on this misty, chilly Saturday morning. The nests all fall to the ground. We bring out a little brazier and with the aid of a shovel throw the worm nests on the fire and quickly duck back inside to avoid any toxic fumes. I can taste the poison on my tongue as the smoke beats me to the kitchen door.

The *processionarios* are *basta*—finished. Our friends from Milan tell us that *processionarios* ARE serious, so I guess it isn't just folklore. Richard and I look around at other Roman pines as we drive to Orvieto, and we can't see any *processionario* nests on them. A few months ago, I was blissfully unaware of such strange things.

"Do you think that all these tree owners get permits too?" I say to Richard. Who would ever have thought that I would be looking at beautiful trees and thinking these thoughts of nasty worms?

"All the neighbors will be very pleased that we have rid them of this pest. Signora Morelli was despised for never having done this!" Vincenzo says.

"How much do we owe you?" I ask Federico our hunter.

"Five Euros" is the reply, demonstrating even further the crassness of Signora Morelli's attitude.

18

MORE WORK MEANS MORE WORKMEN

Per ardua ad alta! (By hard work, to the heights!)
(Roman proverb)

We are at the *bottega* of the blacksmith in Orvieto. He has made us a stunning wrought-iron headboard from a photo I gave him. It is the focus of our master bedroom. It compliments well the old armoire, the beamed ceilings, and the terracotta ceiling tiles. This time we are here to ask him to make a big grid to cover our *pozzo*—it is better that no one can fall down the well. It will look like a grille in some ancient prison, and perhaps provide a great place to put disobedient children. He is also making a window for the *pozzo* to keep out all the damp air that is streaming into the kitchen from the gaping hole that Mario tore to get at the well. He is in his fifties, has fair skin and blue eyes and is reputed to be the son of an occupying German soldier in World War II. He has the German characteristic of being extremely punctual—a welcome relief in this *laissez-faire* world of rural Italy. He has cleverly suggested that he make a small door in the cover for the well so that we will be able to get down to it without removing the whole grid, just like a Jack in the Box. One day we will have a digging party, but there are more pressing issues at hand, namely ensuring some decent living conditions. When we have a party, of course, Mario will be the honored guest, for if he had not noticed the swoosh of cold air and the variance in the wall, our well would have gone undiscovered for another five hundred years.

I'm starting to get anxious to move a little faster on our habitation. It's hard knowing so little about the country and the area, and with my limited Italian, getting a point across is always cumbersome. I get the sense that things will move when they will move, and that I need to take a walk in the morning, perhaps to the bar, and instead of asking for a cappuccino to get me going ask for a *caffe corretto*—a "corrected" coffee, which means coffee with a shot of cognac or any other alcohol in it. I imagine that there is nothing like a good shot of cognac first thing in the morning to knock you off your feet and send you back to bed.

Chapter 18

I remember my visit to the new villa up the road and our abortive attempt through these people to secure workmen. They did mention, though, I recall, that there is a marble guy in the nearby town of Bagnoregio who would perhaps make my kitchen counters in the wonderful local slate-gray *basaltina* to match our original old kitchen fireplace. Not knowing where to start, I get in the car and decide to go to the motherlode, namely the quarry. Its siren for lunch blasts every day across the valley, and so I make my way towards the sound. I drive down a driveway behind a very well-trimmed mile-long hedge at the side of the road, and with horror look at a huge black hole in the earth. It is like the entry to hell—it may have gotten Dante started on writing his *Inferno*. This hillside has been ravaged by everybody from the Romans on. In Roman times, the Tiber River (now a little stream in these parts) was navigable up to the Calanchi Valley, and much of the stone used to make the monuments in Rome comes from this quarry.

A lone worker tells me that, yes, there is a man who does very nice *basaltina* work in town. His name is Renzo. I should look for him, he says, at the town pizzeria. He has a big appetite, he tells me (this is a euphemism) and can always be found at lunchtime at this pizzeria. I guess this is the Italian form of looking for someone in the Yellow Pages.

I have no problem picking Renzo out in the pizzeria. He looks like someone who can lift large slabs of marble and would be a good match for Mario in the World Wrestling Championships. He is sitting in front of a huge pizza and swilling it down with some wine. He says he will come to our house. We'll see.

Today Gloria is cleaning, and her sons are playing in the back garden. This is not her strong suit. I bite my lip. Mario is redelivering our refrigerator; the refrigerator that I bought proved defective after one week's use. The store manager insisted on sending someone out to fix it. Mario was in a fury. With adrenaline pumping through his blood, he picked up the faulty refrigerator almost single-handed, dumped it into his truck, and deposited it in front of the cash register at the store. He had the aura of a participant in a pro wrestling match, or a modern-day Guelph about to start a new war with the Ghibellines.

"The Signora bought a *new* refrigerator, *so*," says Mario, coal-black eyes glaring across the counter, "give the Signora a *new* one."

The assistant doesn't even argue. She gives a peep of a "*Sì*" and tells him to come back for a new one after lunch.

Gloria hears her younger son telling the older son that he had better not use those bad words, as the Cousin of the Virgin Mary may hear and then we would really get into very big trouble. It's good to be so influential.

Things are progressing...slowly. It's spring, and everyone has a lot to do. Signora Gaspari appears with fresh eggs and Agostino appears with fresh spinach. You can judge the seasons by the gifts.

A week has gone by and Renzo the marble guy has not shown up. I go to have my hair cut and the hairdresser Anna tells me the latest village news. "Did you know," she says, "that Renzo greatly injured himself with terrible burns after a gas *bombola*"—canister—"blew up in his workshop?"

I'm not sure how the hairdresser knew that Renzo was meant to be working for me. It seems unlikely to be one of the usual excuses why workmen should not show up. This is the best excuse I have yet heard, next to the one I heard from the tile guy who said, "I can't come today because I am a part-time firefighter and a fire may be breaking out today."

"Yes," says Anna the hairdresser, "they brought in a helicopter and lifted him all the way to Viterbo Hospital, and they say he will never work again with all the terrible burns, especially on his arm."

It all sounds dire.

Anna takes her time with my hair, and I look at my watch and realize it is six o'clock. The local electrician is meant to be arriving at my house that very minute. Anna solves the problem and asks for help from a man who is waiting patiently to have his hair cut. Would he please go to the Signora's house (about a three-minute walk) and please to bring the electrician here to the hairdresser shop to kindly speak to the Signora?

Off he trots, a little mystified, and in five minutes is back in the salon with the electrician, who is more than a little mystified.

A week or two goes by, and a severely damaged Renzo arrives on my doorstep. His burned arm is exposed to the air, making me pleased I haven't just had lunch. He has his sidekick and his young wife in tow. His wife is flapping around him, taking dabs with a cloth at his brow and then his wounded arm. He has horror stories. It looks to me as though he should have had skin grafts. He assures me that with his sidekick doing the heavy work, he will manage, and I'll soon be blessed with a very smart *basaltina* counter to top my gaping kitchen cabinets, which have arrived right on time from the carpenter in Canale.

A week goes by again. I call Renzo, and call and call... nothing happens. So I try the old pizzeria trick, but it's closed today. I storm in a fury to his workshop, which is accessed through a vineyard and down an old rutted road past a picturesque field of sunflowers. I find no Renzo here; I think he got word that I was coming and was probably hiding under a workbench. I really let loose at two of his workers who are polishing a couple of tombstones.

Word goes around town that the Signora is *arrabiata*—furious—and fortunately it is not long before we see action. The job is quickly and beautifully done.

David has arrived from the USA. He is rather aghast at my tyrannical approach, but he acknowledges that, in this climate, his Chairman-of-the-Board style is not going to work.

19

VA CON DIO, GIUSEPPE

A man who feeds men is a man indeed!

The *Cimitero*—cemetery—is not particularly old, particularly given the antiquity of this town; here, the Romans were the newcomers. Gloria tells me that up until about a hundred and fifty years ago Italians could only bury bones and not bodies. The oldest grave is from the late 19th century, but as in all Italian cemeteries, when you look around, everyone seems to live well into their eighties. In contrast, though, I do note that the people born in the middle nineteenth century didn't survive much past their seventies.

Stranger still, the generation that endured two world wars has survived well into their eighties and nineties. Does this mean that deprivation extends life?

We will see where the next generation takes the cemetery.

This morning I'm in the sitting room enjoying the bright sunlight streaming in, the view of Civita ever present in the distance. Fruit trees are now in full blossom, and the scent is quite tantalizing. I look down towards my feet through the French doors looking out onto the street. Right at my feet is a coffin.

Richard and I had heard a painfully slow clanging of the church bell. The tone is so dolorous, its mournfulness is quite clear to any ear.

"For whom the bell tolls..." Richard says poetically.

The coffin, covered in flowers, is in a rather smart glass hearse. Trailing behind, like a sluggish brown river, mourners flow silently. Most of the people look as though they have just stepped off a ladder in an olive grove. The men all walk with their hands behind their backs.

Gloria, my never-ending source of information, says that it is the funeral of the ninety-seven-year-old accountant. He worked all his life for the last Marchesa of the Monaldi, who was the previous owner of the palace. His wife is walking right behind the coffin. They had probably been married around seventy years. What a hard day for this lady. At least he is buried in a beautiful country churchyard.

I think of Grey's *Elegy*: "The ploughman homeward plods his weary way/And leaves the world to darkness and to me."

The road is so narrow in front of our house, and it's the only way to get to the cemetery. Life and death flow past. There is no escaping.

Things change; nothing stays the same.

Two days later we arrive home from a shopping trip to Orvieto to see Gloria's head peeking around the corner of our gate. She has polish in hand and is pretending to shine the gate, but quite obviously she is there to monitor our return.

She says "I am most sad to give you the terrible news that your friend Giuseppe from Vecchio Mulino Restaurant died last night."

Dave and I are in complete disbelief. Just the day before, we had lunch at Giuseppe's restaurant. We arrived at the restaurant well after 2 p.m. and were happy to see the keys in the door. These keys are a simple Lubriano sign to say, "Yes, I am open, and please come in." We were the only people in the restaurant, and we spent quite a bit of time joking with Giuseppe. I wonder in retrospect if he wasn't feeling well yesterday, as he only had two items on the menu rather than the usual eight or ten. He looked exactly the same as ever, clad in the same old sweater that he wore day in and day out. His *Carabaccia* and *Pappardelle al Cinghale* were his last menu choices. As always, they were simply heavenly. He waved us goodbye at about 3:15 p.m.

That night he had a heart attack and died at age sixty-one. "He had no warning," Marisa, his widow, says. "He died without pain."

He leaves behind his wife and four children, including a severely handicapped son who is confined to a wheelchair. We never knew Giuseppe had this son. Sadly, the proud Tuscan must have felt ashamed; he must have kept him behind the old, dark door in the ancient part of the village.

I have no idea how to respond to the mourning. Gloria, who is my eyes and ears in this town, tells me that I should pay my respects to his wife. I cautiously enter her very small, dark apartment and offer a photo taken by a friend from Los Angeles. It is of Giuseppe and Marisa, taken just the week before. This sets her off in floods of tears as she cradles the photo to her breast.

I walk to the little plant and flower shop at the edge of town to order flowers from our family. From under a pile of fertilizer, the owner takes a huge yellow ribbon. It is at least a yard long and three inches wide. She writes our names at least two inches high in black letters on the ribbon. I take the flowers to the church and place them by the altar as we wait for Giuseppe's coffin to be brought in. There is no surreptitious squinting to see who the wreaths are from, as everyone's names in bold black letters are screaming past the flowers and into the congregation.

The church bells ring lugubriously again, a dirge for all who will pass this way. Don Luigi, the priest, whispers a soft, short, service, and the coffin is removed from the church and taken back to the hearse. We all solemnly walk behind, following Giuseppe on his way to the cemetery, the men with hands clasped behind their backs. We walk past our house on this, the only way to the cemetery. I look up, and I see things now from both sides.

The priest leads the mourners to the *cimitero*, and when all are assembled around the grave, to my surprise, Don Luigi quietly slips away back to the church. No last rites, no blessing, nothing. I feel bad, mourning my lost *Carabaccias* and *Pappardelle al Cinghale*, and I can't bear to look at the restaurant as I drive by. The food is intermingled with my thoughts of Giuseppe. My fragrant memory is hard to separate from the man.

20

LORD OF THE FLEAS

Get ye gone, foul pestilence! (Richard Armstrong)

I cook Pork Roast tonight. I cook it with fennel, Orvieto Classico wine, red bell peppers, olive oil, onions, and garlic (*recipe page 329). It simmers away on the stove for about three hours. In the meanwhile, Richard cooks his specialty, *Zucchini Tamburi Neri*, which are little charred drums (*recipe page 275). We munch on these while we are waiting for the roast to finish.

Finally, I thicken the pork roast with a little cream and Parmesan cheese just before serving. Richard and I fall upon the *Maiale in Casseruola*.

Richard has not been happy today. He probably is wondering why he is here while his dad is back home, sitting behind a desk, handing out orders to all his staff; meanwhile, Richard is here amongst a pile of unwelcome construction dust. He is receiving orders from me with not very much enthusiasm. At least he can blame me for his not getting down to writing his book. We have worked hard all afternoon and evening as we gradually inch forward at Braccioforte. Richard would have more success if he had pursued his writing.

Signora Gaspari—oops, Pasquina!—is mystified by Richard's profession. She stopped me yesterday and said she had been thinking about it, and she doesn't see how Richard could be a writer because he doesn't speak very good Italian. "No, he is writing the book in *Inglese*," say I. She gives me a look of complete disbelief. You can see her thinking to herself, "Why would anyone want to write a book in English?"

Anyway, I'm leaving tomorrow to get back to my American life. I'll leave Richard to his foreman and writing problems. I know that he is probably very happy to see the back of me.

The last item on the shopping list before flying back to the USA is to buy a shovel. Richard will not have a car for the next three weeks while I'm gone. A shovel is not usually my last purchase before heading back to the USA; it's usually some truffle oil, a ceramic piece, or a tile or a scarf, but definitely not a shovel. It is going to be hard to leave this place. Life has taken on its own rhythm very different from my life in

Colorado; from today there will be no relaxed stroll down the road to the bar for my café latte.

The construction dust is still around me. I think Lubriano people are going to call me The Dusty Lady of Roma Lane. I seem to have a perpetual layer of white dust coating me, which has the advantage of making me blend in with the farm workers.

At 6 a.m. an old man and his buddy opposite us leave the house with heavy boots and thick wool caps on their heads, off to cultivate their plots of rich earth on the edge of town. In Denver people would be rushing to their cars, clutching cell phones and coffee mugs. I see the two *anziani*—very old men—coming home about 6 p.m. in the evening plod, plod, plod, dusty and dirty from honest labor and suffering no rush-hour stress. So dust can be a badge of honor. I doubt if the construction dust all over my suitcase will be viewed as such when I get to the Denver airport tomorrow.

I'm sad to leave my son Richard behind. In spite of his funk, he is a very comfortable person. I buy him all the ingredients to make his favorite dish tonight after I have gone. I buy a wonderful jar of *Tartufata*, which is a mixture of porcini mushrooms and truffles. Later on, with the stress out of his life, he can settle down to cook *Fettucine Tartufata* with Butter and Parmesan (*recipe page 297).

We make the drive to the town of Bagnoregio, five miles away, heading to the little hardware store to pick up the shovel. I tell Richard we are off to visit the "Shorts." The name of the hardware store is

Gambacorta, which means "short legs." This Lilliputian Home Depot is on a medieval square not thirty feet away from the Church of Saint Nicola. Encased for viewing within the church is a holy relic. Ironically, the relic is half of an arm—a "short arm"—removed some centuries ago from Saint Bonaventura. So here we have *braccio corto*—the short arm—which resides across the square from *gamba corta*—the short-legged hardware store. I tell Gloria that I am going to visit the Shorts, and she is not amused. She is very Catholic in her reverence for the body parts of saints. I'll reserve this humor for my *Protestanti* friends.

Richard and I have been noticing that we always seem to be covered with bites after working in our little guest cottage—the *annesso*—in the garden. Our friendly neighborhood cat is no longer visiting, so we can't blame the bites on her. I suggest we ask in the hardware store for some kind of a flea bomb to fix the matter. This tiny shop sells everything from the usual hardware supplies to bicycles and hiking boots.

It's a very traditional shop. If you are in there shopping and the priest walks in, the entire staff stops serving the customers and serves the priest ahead of everyone. Don Luigi doesn't seem to get the Biblical admonition that "the first shall be last and the last shall be first."

I park illegally while Richard runs into Gambacorta Hardware Store to ask for an insecticide for *pulce*—fleas. He soon returns, having encountered no priest, saying that they have sent him down the road to solve the flea problem. He is hardly gone two minutes and comes back empty-handed, looking angry. The man in the hardware store has sent him to a *profumeria*—a beauty supply shop. When Richard said "*pulce*," the woman running the shop gave him some flea shampoo for himself. Richard is most embarrassed to think that the man in the hardware store and the lady in the *profumeria* thought he himself was infested with fleas. Richard also doesn't think it very funny. I laugh until I have tears running down my face as Richard storms back to the hardware store to tell them that *he* does *not* have fleas, but our cottage does. I don't really think anyone cared either way.

We buy a few cans of insect killer and head back to Braccioforte to send the fleas in the same directions as the toxic *processionarios*—*basta* and *finito*.

I arrive home in Denver to culture shock, and from the first day I set foot in our American home I am hankering to get back to Lubriano and complete the restoration of our Italian home.

21

A WINTER'S TALE

*Now is the winter of our discontent, made glorious
summer by a slice of pork!
(Apologies to William Shakespeare)*

As a girl in my teens, I attended a boarding school in South Africa. It was the early sixties. St. Anne's Diocesan College was in the midlands of Kwa Zulu/Natal. The school was modeled after the Victorian British public school tradition, and long after draconian measures had been abolished in the mother country, we in the colonies were still being subjected to Oliver Twist-type rules. We were taught to keep a stiff upper lip no matter what. No sissy stuff for us!

Even though in winter we used to wake to frost on the ground, we were never allowed to close our bedroom windows—something about Florence Nightingale saving the Crimean troops with fresh air. We slept with the big sash windows open. A generally untried benefit to sleeping in such extreme cold is that, if you can get warm and toasty under mountains of duvets, you can actually have the best sleep of your life.

Here is an example of the school's wonderfully oxymoronic thinking: we school gals were not allowed to wear gloves, even when the temperature was well below 32 degrees Fahrenheit. Due to this absurd rule, some of the girls got the beginnings of frostbite due to poor circulation in the fingers. Only if you got this condition, which was called "chilblains," were you allowed to wear gloves. Little did I know that these privations would prepare me for life in small-town Italy without central heating.

I have new respect for the monks who lived here in Braccioforte a few hundred years ago when it was a monastery.

I also realize that, due to this upbringing, I actually *like* sleeping in a freezing cold room. Two American girlfriends have come back to Italy with me this time. David is still back in America, still talking of retirement. My friends are both longing to get out of this freezer. They are both from warmer climes; Emily is here from Arizona and Jane is here again from California. Jane, with her excellent photographic skills, is in awe of Lubriano. I find her bundled up in the street below taking a photo of a blank wall. In Italy, she says, a wall is never blank; its textures are born from six hundred years of wear. Here a wall can talk to you. Both friends are being stoic, but being this cold is inconceivable to both of them.

Italy is experiencing one of its coldest winters in two hundred years.

It's a bitterly cold night. We go to Trattoria del Pozzo, a restaurant set in the middle of a vineyard on the outskirts of town. You have to be local to find this place. Its great big fireplaces are always on our minds in winter. We receive a warm welcome from owner Deutzia, her husband Pierro, and their son Mauro. Pierro is owner/chef; he is continually hunched over a cooktop or a pasta table. He doesn't look up very often. Richard has gone home to the USA, and Pierro is missing him. So am I. Pierro tells me that he is going to will the restaurant to Richard, as no one in his family understands food like my son does.

Pierro is a fabulous natural cook. He often prepares a dish that sends my taste buds into orbit— Toasted Polenta Squares smothered with a Mushroom, Rosemary, and Sausage Sauce (*recipe page 307).

We have a hearty welcome from all the town people who are eating in the restaurant. A television broadcasts another never-ending game of soccer. Everyone is asking after Richard, who spent so many nights here. The huge wood stove in the middle of the restaurant draws us in. A succulent-looking chicken dish simmers gently atop the huge wood stove— Chicken *Buione* (*recipe page 319). It is chicken done the Lubriano way, Pierro tells us. Chicken pieces, skin on, are left to sauté in a heavy skillet with olive oil, butter, rosemary, and garlic until the chicken is crispy and brown. Wine is then poured over the chicken and the dish simmers longer still, until all the wine too has evaporated. The succulence and aroma of this dish saturate us with good cheer.

Our bones are freezing. There is a marmalade cat lying by the fire with the most peaceful look; joy is flowing out of him and into our hearts. Byron, the golden retriever, has learned to open the door with his paw and barges into the restaurant. Everyone cringes with the new blast of Scandinavian air. The dog flops down by the fire and tucks his nose into the cat.

You may well ask how someone in rural Italy has a dog called Byron. It turns out that Deutzia, Pierro's wife, is a huge fan of Lord Byron. Deutzia's eyes are black and wild as she quotes her muse in perfect English, accompanied, of course, by very Italian hand actions:

"Yet Freedom! Yet thy banner, torn but flying
Streams like the thunderstorm against the
wind!"

Our plumber, who is sitting at the next table, looks at her and us with some mystification.

Tonight Mauro is smiling because his girlfriend is back. We all feel that some Los Angeles scriptwriter used them to model his characters. Mauro is twenty-six years old, while his girlfriend is fifty-five years old (if she's lucky); she is from Beverly Hills. She wins David over by asking how our daughter is. Well, that is what he says won him over. She is quite charming, I must admit, and has an incredible body. Her tight, youthful clothes complete the picture. She rents a villa in the area each summer and leaves her aged and obviously wealthy husband back home while she comes to enjoy some of the other pleasures of *la dolce vita*.

We gather that this relationship has been an ongoing annual summer "thing," punctuated by lots of lovers' spats.

I guess a good arrangement is one in which both parties' needs are met. Mauro's needs happen to be met by being given a gift of an extremely expensive watch, and we won't discuss her needs, but I'm sure they are being met, too.

There is a table of New Zealanders here tonight, parents and three daughters in their twenties. In contrast to the Beverly Hills lover, each young girl looks like she has been tucking into far too much of their dairy cream. Mauro, so handsome in that young Latin way, is hovering with his dreamy eyes. He is being especially courteous, as he always is when waiting on the clientele in the restaurant. He is treating the girls as though they were Paris Hilton and friends. I lean over to the New Zealand family and say, "Isn't he just great?"

Dour looks reply. One daughter says, "Yeeah, but his *ponts* are too *toit*!"

My girlfriends all agree that Mauro's pants could never be too tight.

We have a wonderful meal. We begin with toasty hot and shiny roasted bell peppers served straight from the pizza oven. It's a treat to watch

Pierro cooking. He cuts the peppers into quarters and thrusts them into the pizza oven for a few minutes. They come out a beautiful brown. Then, and only then, he drizzles a little olive oil over them. They have an outstanding texture, free of the sliminess characteristic of peppers roasted in oil in a regular oven. We have thinly sliced *prosciutto* and creamy *fagioli*—cannellini beans—soft and buttery and served in olive oil, rosemary, and garlic. This is followed by steamed fennel baked in the oven with a béchamel sauce. Then comes the toasted polenta, served with a sauce made with porcini mushrooms, cream, and sausage. At this stage we try to call an end to this madness, but there is no stopping the *secondi*—the main course. Three separate dishes arrive: Rosemary Roasted Pork Chops, the Chicken *Buione* we have longed for all evening, and Veal *Scallopine* (*recipe page 339). All these are served with Pierro's Slow-Roasted Onions topped with Crispy Breadcrumbs (*recipe page 345).

Our stomachs are groaning. With just a little bit of this and a little bit of that, we have each probably taken in enough calories for an entire week. After all this food frenzy, the *dolce* of *Panna Cotta* arrives, along with Fresh Figs and *Limoncello* Liqueur (*recipe page 355).

Sweet Lord, preserve us from this gluttony!

It's hard to leave this earthly version of Dante's *Paradiso*, where life is reduced to the essentials of warmth and affection, and step out into a dimly lit parking lot. The parking area is hastily constructed around a huge old chestnut tree scuffed by too many hasty bumpers.

We fly through the dark country lanes, hoping the fire at home has some embers left for us.

The chill in the village in Lubriano seems to pour down Via Roma at just the spot between our casa and where we park our car, and it's a huge test to run the distance from the car to Braccioforte with our fire in mind.

As we park the car in the square we can hear the chants of the Friday night Adoration service in the church, so we sneak in and take a seat in the shadows of the candlelight. Saints and angels slip in and out of the light. The lady taking the collection unabashedly peers into the plate as I throw my donation in. They switch the church heating off when the service begins. Everyone is wrapped up in their winter coats, hats pulled down low and scarves pulled up high. "*Vieni, Vieni,*" the people sing over and over. The service lilts on in sweet musical tones, over and over and over, until you slip into your own brand of peaceful, warm, subconscious prayer.

We catch the last warmth of our kitchen fire, toes hard up against the dying logs, a grappa or two in hand, while Andrea Bocelli lulls us. I bless myself for remembering earlier to put hot water bottles in our beds.

☙❧

We call the fireplace "Lubriano Television."

Before we leave the kitchen, I think how pleased everyone will be if I make Tuscan Beans on the fire overnight (*recipe page 309). My friends look at me as though this life is turning me a little *pazza*—crazy. Unfazed, I pull an old Chianti wine flask out of the closet, filling it with a cup of dried small white beans, cloves of garlic, a big bunch of fresh sage, olive oil, and water. I stop up the flask and place it in the dying fire, then mound some coals around the flask and head for bed.

Also tonight, I have made my favorite breakfast for my guests. I call it my *Frittata*. It is a combination of many little leftovers from previous meals. I layer stale bread on the bottom of a pan, then scoop in some grilled vegetables, some pancetta, a few chopped tomatoes, and a good dollop of cream here and there. I chop oregano and parsley and sprinkle it on top. Then I gently whisk the eggs and pour them on top. In the morning I will bake it with some shavings of fresh Parmesan (*recipe page 287).

It's hard to get up in the chill of the morning, but the thought of my buttery beans huddling in the fire jumpstarts me. I wander down the stairs from my bedroom. Every riser is a different height; every step I take is a surprise, and my cold feet don't want to bend.

The kitchen is still damp. Gloria insists we have a spring under our kitchen; she has visions of bottling Braccioforte Sparkling Water.

Being a good host, I attack the chill of the kitchen and immediately head for the *basaltina* fireplace in the corner. It is black with several centuries' worth of fires. There is a little glow coming from the charred logs. The beans are soft and creamy and still warm. I shake them from the flask for serving tonight. I stay long enough to get the fire going and scamper back to bed with my espresso. I can hear Agostino slaving away, building a small retaining wall outside in the bare elements with just a shirt on—and a dress shirt, no less.

The kitchen is one huge refrigerator; we are in the process of getting our electricity upgraded. It is good to get the oven on. I take out the *frittata* and slide it into the welcome heat. At the moment, we have to choose between leaving the space heaters on in the bedrooms and leaving the water heaters on all night for a nice warm morning bath. We certainly have all the electrical equipment, but not the necessary number of watts coming in to run them all at the same time. With true Italian back-to-front thinking, Gloria tells me if I apply for more electrical current I'll be refused, but if I buy a lot of appliances and then complain, I'll get more electric current added.

ॐॐ

We feel the need to leave the house after so many days of sitting and watching the fire, so we wander off towards Montefiascone. It is a wonderful town on Lake Bolsena that has a cathedral with the third largest dome in Italy after St. Peter's and the

Duomo in Florence—the Cathedral of St. Margherita. The church is fifteenth century and the dome is seventeenth century. The inside of the dome is frescoed in classical Florentine tradition.

This church is perched up on the highest hill and can be seen for about eighty miles around, from every point in the Alto Lazio and southern Umbria and also from southern Tuscany. We soon realize that it is not a good choice to visit the highest point in the region on this bitterly cold, windy day.

We three look starched stiff as we come upon the cathedral doors, for we are nearly swept off our feet. With astoundingly accurate timing, a little curator opens the church door at the moment I put my hand on its frozen brass knob. I suspect that he has a remote camera and has watched us battling up to the pinnacle against the wind. He is a modern-day Quasimodo.

Since we are the only people stupid enough to venture out today, Quasimodo gives us our own personal tour. He leads us down a dark, dimly lit tunnel of a staircase into the bowels of the church. A lady is serenely lying there in a glass coffin. Santa Lucia is a new saint from about 150 years ago and has her own order of nuns in New Jersey. Her crypt is most impressive, and quite modern given the fifteenth-century church above. This crypt was only built in the nineteen sixties, in contrast to the elaborately decorated church and dome above, which have been there since the Renaissance. Down here, everything is modern.

Chapter 21

Quasimodo makes us all stoop down low and peer, at a most unbecoming angle, to see the face of the saint. We are a little squeamish about coming face-to-face about six inches away from a dead body, but it is required by this curator. Who knows? If we don't, he may never let us upstairs again.

After this chilly start to the day, we set off for the fishing village of Marta on the southern edge of beautiful Lake Bolsena. The winding road to Marta from Lubriano is full of green, rolling farms with many flocks of sheep. There is always one black sheep in each flock here. Roman pines string the hillsides. Some fields are plowed heavily, with tilled terracotta-colored earth lying in huge ridges.

I wonder to myself if these pines have *processionarios* too. I also wonder if Italians come to the USA looking for *processionarios* in our pines.

The waves are whipping off the lake, but the sun is shining, making the water aqua blue. All the restaurants that line the picturesque Marta waterfront are closed but one. We sprint to find a warm, cozy, cheery interior. We order *Fruiti di Mare Fritto Misto*, a mixed fish platter with little lightly fried white bait, calamari, and prawns. This is served with a *primi* of *Fettucine con Funghi Porcini*—Fettucine with Porcini Mushrooms. The porcini are cooked very lightly and tossed into the cream sauce with just a hint of garlic and lemon.

෨ඁ෨

Ahhh! At last, today is a little warmer. The valley below is shining in the morning light. I wander down past the three big, shallow water troughs where the women of years gone by washed their laundry. The town of Civita is reflected in the water. The troughs have obviously been used recently, as the middle trough is quite soapy, which makes the water look a milky blue in the morning light. The reflection in these three troughs makes a triptych reflection of Civita.

I come across a completely new view of Lubriano. If you look up at Lubriano from the valley, the village looks like a twin city of Civita as it strings out along the ridge. In a long silhouette, I see the oldest structure in Lubriano, the eleventh-century *torre*—tower—standing high, and the church steeple, and then look along the ridge past our house where the cliff by the cemetery drops off into the valley below. From here, looking up at Lubriano, the town takes on a different aspect. I'm reminded of looking out my window and seeing that coffin gliding by, and then the next week being in Giuseppe's funeral procession and looking up at my window. I make a mental note always to try to look at things from both sides.

I go home and rally our houseguests for a picnic in my newfound spot. The chilly winds that blow into our back garden can't get down into this valley, and it's warm and peaceful down here with the sheep grazing, chickens clucking, and the faint sound of the people in the church singing the Lord's Prayer.

Chapter 21

One has to have come to Lubriano a few times to realize that there is a road down into the valley, winding precipitously down through a small opening in a buttress wall. The road drops right off the edge and cascades into the valley below. It's hard to believe that a road meanders down there. It is another day of clear blue that reminds me of Colorado. *Il postino*—the mailman—is washing his car right on a perilous corner. He kindly pulls aside a wheelbarrow sitting in the middle of the road so that our car can pass.

We set up the picnic under a fig tree and near some olives. We spread a couple of blankets and flop down, looking up onto the bright silver underside of the olive leaves. Yesterday we stopped at a farm with a pretty significant cheese factory where we bought a wheel of sweet *pecorino*—sheep's milk cheese. One of the cheese factory workers happened to have a cigarette dangling out of the corner of his mouth as he was stacking the wheels of cheese for storage. Putting this thought aside, we cut the first slices and silence reigns. From this angle the sky looks even bluer. We have brought a merlot wine from the local winery Pazzaglia; it is a pale, clear ruby color in the sunlight. Along with the *pecorino* cheese, we eat thick honey—I love the combination. We have a salad with just-picked arugula and a delicate fresh ham called *Prosciutto Cotto*. Our bread is still warm from the bakery at the top of the hill.

To our amazement, a sheep gives birth to twin lambs about fifty feet away from us. An attendant midwife sheep is bleating in encouragement. The rest

157

of the flock keeps its distance.

I wander down the steep incline with the sheep safely grazing by the road. In the distance I see an old man at the top of a ladder, high up in an olive tree. He is busily pruning. With a giant swoosh, branches fall to the ground. With the sharp winter sun cutting through the valley, I pick up my camera and focus on the man; I bring him into my telescopic view. It is Agostino, one of our trusty workers. For the past couple of weeks he has been working for me six days a week.

"*La Stampa*," I call out. I have heard that in town this is his nickname which means "party animal."

He chuckles and looks at me coyly. This is his day of rest, but he is up in an olive tree. I wander across the field to chat with him. The olive trees sitting in this beautiful valley belong to a friend, he says.

Full of warmth and sunshine, we leave the valley for home. Gloria is there. She says it's better to bump into Agostino in the valley than near his house. "The road to his house," she says, "is steep and dangerous, and he has two dogs that act very friendly and welcome you to the house, but when you leave they snarl and hold you captive."

She asks us to come over for a lunch of Lasagna with Porcini Mushrooms after Mass, as Mario has bought far too many porcini mushrooms and cheese. The lasagna is, as always, amazing, but could not be higher in fat or calories, with its lashings of cream and butter baked in (*recipe page 305). In my mind, I hear a friend in Denver saying, "What's not to like?" True. But my friend here at the lunch table is from Phoenix and is trying to fit into a dress for a wedding. She doesn't look pleased at the massive, buttery platter in front of her. I try to make up for her lack of enthusiasm by overeating. People who come to Umbria in winter should be warned that hearty Umbrian cooking is not compatible with fitting into clothes for weddings.

I roll home ponderously from lunch. We have invited a neighbor for tea. My brain is addled by the food I ate for two people. We sit in the sun in the *salone* with the fresco looking down at us and our English scones. The room is filled with sunlight and we are warm. Today is the first day we unglued ourselves from the kitchen fire. I feel, sitting here in the *salone*, that I have abandoned an old friend.

☙❧

Today Gloria tells me that it's going to snow tonight because some crows have arrived. This is probably more accurate than Weather.com's forecasts for Orvieto. Perhaps it's the calm before the storm, because today is a perfect day. We wander down into the valley again to sit under one of Agostino's well-pruned trees.

It's good to now feel warm again for we have been going through what I call "*Survivor* Lubriano." We started off here on arrival from London with little heat, then the big break came when the electric company piped more electricity into the house, but it's still a juggling act to have all four water heaters on at once. I think my two friends would be happy to be voted off and flown home to their warm houses in the USA.

Jane, being from Los Angeles, is wishing it would snow. I am from Denver and am wishing it would NOT. Jane says, "At least, if you are going to be this cold, you should have something to show the folks back home."

We are sitting in a restaurant in Orvieto, *I Sette Consoli.* It is situated in an old cellar, so we are completely shielded from the elements. I get a frantic call from Gloria.

"You see? I was right about the crows," she cries with obvious glee. "You should come home immediately, because all the roads in Lubriano are frozen and full of snow, and if you don't come home now you will never ever get home."

We think, "There goes Gloria, dramatizing again." Nevertheless, we pay the bill and quickly leave the restaurant. This is really hard to do, as we have ordered a warm pear tart and cream.

We go out and can hardly believe our eyes, it is snowing so hard. The massive Orvieto cathedral is barely visible for the large snowflakes that are falling. Already a large amount of snow has accumulated on my car. We carefully set off for home, and notice a man putting chains on his car.

"Oh! These Italians overreacting again," I say.

A little further up the hill towards the highlands on which Lubriano sits, we come upon a long line of cars stranded by the side of the road. There are a couple of trucks jack-knifed, as if to prove me wrong about Italians overreacting. The vineyards are laden with snow and the olive trees are at the breaking point with snow weighing down their boughs. A flock of sheep scurries across the road as a farmer shepherds them to a more sheltered spot. Our usual twenty-minute drive takes two hours. With lots of experience driving in Denver and a great deal of pushing from my poor friends, we barrel on by the trucks littering the sides of the *strada*. I'm studiously ignoring the smell of burning clutch as I ride it all the way home.

Lubriano looks like a Christmas card, and the view is even more spectacular than usual, with the fairy-tale city of Civita rising, snow-covered, out of the valley. The mood of the town is one of disbelief. One Lubrianese is in particular disbelief. He lives on the corner of Via Marconi and Via Roma and is staring, aghast, at the Mercedes embedded in his house.

Jane prayed too hard for snow. There is way too much snow.

༒

It is the day of David's arrival and the pipes in the *annesso* are frozen. This is the last time David will be commuting back and forth. I am excited as he is just a few months away from retiring. He arrives from

Fiumicino Airport via Max in his limousine, as always with his complaints. David is completely amazed at the snow-blanketed village.

I have taken a space heater outside and put it in the garden with its heat blowing against the water pipes leading into the little guest cottage. I'm sure our Italian neighbors have confirmed their suspicions that I am really batty. Mario was the person who ran the water line into the little cottage, and I have unhappy thoughts of having to dig up the garden to sink his hasty plumbing job deeper into the earth.

David is mystified by the blasting heater in the garden propped in the snow, as though I'm singlehandedly trying to add to global warming. My brother is coming later on the train from Rome. When he calls, I tell him I can't pick him up and to please take a taxi from the Orvieto train station to Lubriano. He sounds suspicious. Of course, in order to prove me an exaggerator, by the time he arrives things are somewhat back to normal, with just some residual snow lying on the olive trees. The pipes, in the comparative warmth of the late morning and probably not as a result of my heater, have unfrozen.

We settle down to my Braccioforte Rosemary Vegetable soup (*recipe page 287), my standard welcome dish for tired and hungry travelers. I have a secret herb mixture that I gather from the garden at the end of summer, when rosemary, thyme, sage, and lavender are growing in profusion in all the flower beds. Like inviting an old friend into the kitchen rather than leaving her to the mercies of the unsettled fall, I combine the herbs into a delightful mixture preserved with the best olive oil, fresh lemon juice, and garlic. I blend it into a paste and place the mixture in the freezer in flat plastic bags, and like a bar of chocolate, when I want my spirits lifted, I break a piece off the frozen paste and throw it into soups and stews or slather it onto meats or vegetables ready for the grill.

Tomorrow we will take my brother truffle hunting, so the frozen pipes can be forgotten.

22

BLACK TRUFFLES (FOR BEGINNERS)

Before we can see him, we can hear him. His herald is a *pfutt, pfutt, pfutt,* the sound that comes from neither a scooter nor a car but a small Italian vehicle called an Ape (meaning "bee").

Domenico the truffle hunter is here.

We are relieved to see him with his truffle dog of unknown descent sitting next to him. Both are squeezed into the driver's seat, surrounded by a teensy enclosed compartment no bigger than a good-size cardboard box. The two make an odd sight as they turn the corner into the little village near Assisi.

Domenico, a big calm man with baronial looks, swings open the Ape's door and carefully unpackages himself.

The dog jumps out without looking at us. She has her eyes firmly fixed Domenico's Harris tweed jacket.

It is 8 a.m. on a very chilly February morning.

"Can dogs smell truffles through snow?" my husband asks me, as if I should know.

"Perhaps," I say.

I do know that black truffles form closer to the surface than white ones, but as to dogs' olfactory skills after a six-inch snow fall, I have no clue.

"Black truffles, it is possible to scent with snow, but difficult!" Domenico says.

Domenico hands us each a gnarled old hiking pole and inspects us for sturdy shoes before he crawls back into his Ape to lead us into the white hills.

Truffles can become an obsession. In the Piedmont's Alba region, the home of white truffles, a white truffle the size of a golf ball can sell for far more than Domenico's Ape.

With Domenico and his dog Radda in the lead, we drive off, sliding up the mountain over icy roads. Lower down, in the valley below, there is less snow. Gentle honey-colored fields are fringed with deep green woods. Radda is still staring down at Domenico's jacket.

Domenico scrambles off the path and points into some trees with his truffle iron. "Brava, Radda! Brava!" he whispers in an urgent tone that I presume means "Let the games begin" in truffle dog language.

Radda rushes away from us. She is honey beige with the body of a beagle, the legs of a terrier, and the face of a pointer. She shoves her slim nose deep into the snow, and with lightening speed, she digs.

A skilled truffle hunter obviously needs many skills. One appears to be to stop the dog at the precise moment that the truffle is found so that it is not damaged by pointy claws or eaten by pointy teeth.

But better pointy claws and pointy teeth than snouts. "Pigs, they are too strong, too rough, and they eat the truffle before you can get to it," says Domenico.

"Brava, Radda! Brava!" Domenico praises his dog as he reaches into the snow for the undamaged walnut-sized truffle with one hand and into his jacket pocket with the other. He brings out about three morsels of dog food. Radda has unearthed a black truffle that promises to bring Domenico the equivalent of twenty dollars at market, he says. At three morsels of dog food apiece, if I were a dog I would demand better wages.

He picks up the dog, ruffles her ears, puts the truffle to his nose and then our noses, and then places it in a small cloth bag. As hard as I try, I can never quite carry that truffle scent in my head as I do chocolate or coffee, for instance. The scent is all-pervasive and so distinctive it annoys me not to be able to recall it at will. It is dank and primordial and exciting. Long after the truffle is in the bag, I am left with a buzz that is earthy but at the same time highly perfumed.

"This one is not so aromatic. It should be used only for cooking, not for shaving on top of a dish!" he complains.

And so the hunt goes on. Sometimes Radda shoots off the path and down a steep embankment, and at other times she races across the fields as if in pursuit of a fox.

Domenico tells us that it is difficult to train a dog to hunt truffles. It is very hard to make dogs give up the prize in return for the dog food. This is like asking a toddler to give up his ice cream in return for a green bean.

The sun is getting somewhat stronger, but not melting any snow. By now Domenico has harvested about ten black truffles of different sizes and aromatic levels. The hunt is winding down; our zig-zagging after Domenico, who is zig-zagging after the dog, appears to be less urgent.

Back where we began, it is now 10 a.m. I have to admit to being a little weary after being in constant pursuit of a truffle hunter who himself is in pursuit of his dog. I also have numb feet.

We halt in the middle of the path. Our commander and his dog look fresh, but we are a rag-tag battalion. Domenico pulls out a large flask of coffee. Then he pulls out a flask of brandy.

"*Caffe corretto?*" he offers.

His recipe appears to call for equal parts of coffee and brandy.

My husband, my brother, and I at first refuse, but the aroma is as heady as the truffles. Our heightened senses say with gratification, "*Grazie!*"

Chapter 22

We leave Domenico and Radda, flush with our gift of one good black truffle. The whole car is pungent with the scent of the truffle all the way down from Assisi to our little village. Truffles lose their pungency and mass quickly. I take sniffs of the truffle all the way home, thinking how lucky I am to have this truffle flying at the speed of a Fiat Punto into my pan.

We rush into the kitchen and light a fire. I am going home to cook a simple dinner and let the truffle take over with its not-so-subtle scent.

I'll serve a Grilled Porcini Mushroom (*recipe page 273) as an appetizer, then a small Salad of Finely Shaved Fennel Root, Fennel Fronds, and Apples Drizzled with Lemon Juice and Olive Oil (*recipe page 271), followed by the fresh local Umbrian *Pappardelle* Tossed with Butter and Topped with Shaved Truffles (*recipe page 293), and then finish off the meal with Grilled Figs (*recipe page 347), *Gelato di Crema* (*recipe page 349), and a specialty from the Le Marche region of Italy: *Casciotta con Foglie di Noce* (Aged *Pecorino* Wrapped in Walnut Leaves).

23

THE $6,000 RABBIT

And what rough beast, its hour come round at last,
slouches towards Lubriano to be eaten?
(Apologies to W.B. Yeats)

This $6,000 rabbit is the result of having at last, to acknowledge Signora Gaspari's constant harping about "*Radice, radice*"—roots, roots. So now we have found out that the Gaspari's cantina roof is caving in. Unfortunately their cantina is situated directly underneath our garden. This promises to obliterate their cantina and turn our garden into a sinkhole. Cantinas are basement-caves that were dug out underneath houses (and apparently gardens) many hundreds of years ago and were used for the making and storage of wine and olive oil. The Gasparis have now told us the full story of the roots from our tree above invading their cantina below, causing their ceiling to collapse.

Gloria, of course, has an additional take on it. She says that their ceiling has been dug too high into our garden. Even though Italian law says that the cost of such a repair should be shared, we can see that the Gasparis would never pay for their share of the repair. As we suspected, a visit to view the problem turned the problem into ours.

The words of our very good British friend Peter Dixon who has lived for the past fifteen years in Italy reverberate: "You don't need insurance in Italy. All you need is a jolly good strong door and jolly good relations with your neighbors."

In all honesty, we feel we would be more likely to win the lottery than convince this couple to split the cost with us. We decide to foot the bill for the repair in order to preserve our "good neighbors watching over our property" insurance policy. In fact, Pasquina watches over our place whether we are there or not. Her vigilance extends the full twenty-four hours. "Have a bad night?" Pasquina says in the morning. *So 2 a.m. is on her watch, too,* I think as I head again for a middle-of-the-night glass of milk in the kitchen.

The whole roots thing slowly comes into focus. It appears that the only reason we were able to buy our house at all is because we spoke no Italian at the time. Another neighbor tells us that the Gasparis have been on the lookout for prospective buyers of Signora Morelli's house for years. At the first clink of the gate and a realtor, Pasquina would assail them with the horrendous root problem they would be inheriting. Did they know that they would have this large problem and an enormous bill to deal with should they buy this house? We now know why Signor Galli was so anxious during the walkthrough on the day of our closing: he was about to lose a sale if he even gave Pasquina half a chance.

We engage little old wiry Agostino to fix the cantina. He builds a World War III fortress down there. He is so proud of his work that he has written into the concrete "Agostino Domenici," as if he were Michelangelo signing his name on the Sistine Chapel. Everyone is entirely satisfied with the fortification, and I can finally remove the big flower pots I had placed strategically to avoid losing an unsuspecting houseguest into the earth.

Soon after the completion of the nuclear bunker, Signora Gaspari arrives at our back door with what I like to think is a pang of guilt for not paying their half share of this project.

"Do you like *coniglio?*" she says.

I nod, trying to be polite. I am not really into cooking bunnies. My lovely, gentle daughter Heather and her husband Seth are visiting from Florida with their young children. They are arriving home soon from a day trip to Siena, and I keep taking a look down Via Roma for them with their little brood behind them. I am hoping that their arrival does not coincide with that of a kicking, squealing ball of fluff.

Fortunately Signora Gaspari arrives speedily. With relief, I see that she has a dead, well-skinned, well-dressed rabbit. She is also delivering the rabbit liver, carefully displayed on a plate with a little sage. I immediately hide the lot at the back of the refrigerator and save it for a child-free meal with no likelihood of a "Di what is THAT?" question. Tonight I am cooking a more universally acceptable family favorite, *Pasta e Fagioli* (*recipe page 299), with fresh pasta from the *Pasta Fresca* shop in Orvieto and lots of herbs from my garden.

I call the proffered rabbit "the $6,000 rabbit," for that was the cost of repairing the Gasparis' cantina so that our garden, and those sitting in it, wouldn't fall into the room below. The next day, while the family is visiting Rome, I cook the $6,000 rabbit just as Signora Gaspari has told me to. I brown it on top of the stove in olive oil and garlic, then add a lot of fresh rosemary and sage and some onion and carrot and continue to brown it. When the rabbit is a caramel color, I pour in a cup of wine, add some olives, and then cover it and put it in the oven for two hours (*recipe page 317). Just before serving I add some cream. It's really most succulent—and should be, for such a price!

I cook the rabbit liver my way, as I have cooked chicken, duck, and goose liver for the last thirty years: with a good shot of cognac and some cream and garlic.

Chapter 23

So it is Gasparis, one and Armstrongs, zero. We have the feeling it may always be that way.

"So Erica"—which means "Heather" in Italian—"and the *ragazzi* love to eat rabbit? *Sì?*" says Signora Gaspari.

"*Sì*," I say emphatically. Sometimes one just has to lie.

24

PIZZA IN THE PALACE

I bump into Angelo Giordano, the owner of the palace, at the hardware store. Today he is sporting an Austrian felt hat with a little feather sticking up on the side. This lends him a jaunty air and adds credibility to my notion that he is really Baron von Trapp from *The Sound of Music* in disguise. With an expansive wave of his arm, he invites us to dinner at the palace on Saturday. He is planning a special meal, and adds mysteriously that there will be musical entertainment. His sister Caterina will call us from Rome to explain the arrangements, as it is rather complicated and his English is poor.

Caterina calls a day or two later to confirm the arrangement, and she confides to us that among the other guests are some well-known musicians. This is a most unusual invitation, and we feel very fortunate. An elegant dinner in a palace, with entertainment by famous musicians! Who can they be? Pavarotti? Bocelli? We can hardly believe our luck.

On the appointed evening we are ready to party. David has just flown in from the USA, but with his frequent comings and goings to his office in the USA there is no time to think about jet lag. We set off and walk the hundred yards from our house to the palace. We are admitted through the giant doors and ushered through the grand reception rooms. We are thinking that we will stop in their splendid dining room, but somewhat unexpectedly, we find ourselves in a kitchen. It is one of three kitchens in the palace, they tell us.

To be sure, it is a kitchen unlike any other. The ceilings are at least fifteen feet high. The tiles around the oven are very old, with a curly blue design on antique white. The whole effect is distinctly Moorish, but with overtones of a baronial hall, including a fireplace at the one end that is so large you could stand in it. The room is complete with a chandelier. The focal point of the room is an ancient table, big enough to seat about fifteen people, or maybe twenty. Certainly it is a kitchen in a million, but it is still, well, a kitchen. Would Pavarotti be joining us in the kitchen?

From an adjoining salon, the sounds of music start to swell, and then to swell more! And still more, until the plates start to rattle. It sounds like a rock band. In fact, it *is* a rock band. Thoughts of Pavarotti begin to fade as we realize that the famous musicians we have come to hear are actually an English rock band from Liverpool. (No, not *that* rock band from Liverpool!) We now learn that Caterina is a promoter of rock bands in Italy.

Although a number of kitchen staff are hovering nearby, Angelo himself is making *panini* in the pizza oven. He scoops them out with his paddle and quickly stuffs them with *capocollo*—boar's-head salami—which has been cured and transported from his other palace in Basilicata.

It's time for wine. The staff brings out bottles of red s*pumante* from the Giordano vineyards. The first bottle explodes when Angelo opens it, covering those nearby with a spray of fizzy red bubbles. He laughs and doesn't attempt to wipe the red fizz off himself. He wears it like a badge of honor of the wine-producing classes. He is quite happy to remain spattered with red drops of *spumante* trickling down his forehead!

The party starts to grow, a very familiar occurrence in Italy. Our hosts have eight children, all of whom are in attendance. Then there is the beautiful sister, Caterina, with her architect husband, and a brother from Rome, who is a famous actor, with a couple of his acolytes. They must wonder how on earth these strange Americans found their way into this rarified company. We look around at this eclectic group, gathered in this enormous palazzo in a tiny village in the middle of Italy, and wonder about it too.

Just as we are starting to feel rather comfortable in this grand kitchen, suddenly, with far too many *panini* and *spumantes* under our belts, we are ushered from the pizza kitchen through to the highly frescoed palace dining room.

At the head of the table, waiting for us, sits Angelo's mother, the *Donna*. She glowers down the full length of the table, cigarillo in hand, as the family seat themselves amidst us and the rock group. Despite many hugs and kisses from all her family, the *Donna* refuses to crack a smile. She looks the epitome of a rich *contessa*, with her patrician looks and her beautifully coiffed shock of white hair. I cannot even imagine what she thinks of us Americans and the rock group with their hungover miens and motley attire.

Gloria swaggers in with a piece of paper and takes our orders. She has on her usual slightly disgruntled air, but nobody notices, which disgruntles her a bit more. Each of us will receive a personalized pizza: pizza with eggplant, pizza with arugula and radicchio, pizza with gorgonzola, pizza with buffalo mozzarella and fresh tomatoes, and lastly pizza with pasta on the top, but this last one has no takers.

In the kitchen, Mario is putting his skills to work, and since he is a former pizza-man from Naples, these skills are formidable. Somewhat surprisingly, our host, Angelo, is in the kitchen too, working *gomito a gomito*—elbow to elbow—with his pizza-man. About twenty different pizzas are ordered, and in short order they start streaming into the dining room. Angelo helps the kitchen ladies. We are amused to see the he is still wearing a splash of red *spumante* on his forehead.

We each try our own pizzas and then take a slice of each others'. We can hardly keep up, but they are delicious, so we keep on eating. And eating. And eating.

Finally our hostess, Carmela, heralds the end of the meal with a really huge *torta*—a tart. It is an apple and honey tart not much smaller than a bicycle wheel. On the side, Gloria quietly slips in her special— a *tiramisu*. She has the air of an English butler who, though at first appearing subservient, wields superiority over the master. Carmela, meanwhile, looks stunning standing there with her huge *torta*. She is a beautiful woman and hardly looks as though she has eight children. It goes without saying that we don't make much of a dent in the desserts.

While we are attempting to eat dessert the musicians drift off, then music begins swelling through the reception rooms. Feet start tapping. Heads bob to the beat. As one, we all stand up, drawn to the throb of the distant music. The sound is coming from the ballroom. Carmela leads the impromptu conga line, rocking and rolling to the music. She has a wine glass held up high. We all follow along the corridors and through grand halls towards the sound.

The ballroom is huge and grand. Oil paintings and tapestries line the walls. I have a fleeting feeling that Pavarotti would feel quite at home here. But instead, the promised rock band is there, in full battle dress. Their equipment fills one end of the room. Speakers, amplifiers, an industrial-strength drum kit, and coils of electric speaker cables are arrayed incongruously under a giant chandelier. Their music has a strikingly universal appeal—no wonder they have such a big following in Italy! The ballroom rocks as everyone dances. Well, everyone except the dour matriarch, of course.

An open mike is announced. In America, few of our friends would dare to sing in public, especially in front of a professional band, but this, after all, is Italy, and there are a number of guests ready to strut their stuff. All eight of the Giordano children take a turn at the mike, and it turns out that all eight of them really know how to sing. Again I have the fleeting feeling that we are channeling the von Trapps here!

Hours go by, and the party never flags. But finally we manage to pull ourselves away. Angelo is protesting that the party is just beginning. Their eight children line up to wish us goodnight. We are half expecting a sung *"Auf Wiedersein,"* but instead there are farewell bear hugs and kisses all round, leaving us in no doubt that we are well and truly in Italy.

25

COMPLIMENTI DAVID

As that great host with measured tread,
Rolled slow towards the bridge's head...
(Macaulay)

David has finally taken the big step and retired. It is a great relief to both of us. After being a bystander and check writer in the world of Italian house restoring, he is about to gain firsthand experience of what it means to be a member of the Braccioforte construction crew. Quite frankly, I hope that once he gets a taste of it, he won't head straight back for the boardroom.

He has had a long, busy, all-consuming career. He has worked and I have moved house! Our twelve moves have spanned two continents and taken in almost every sector of the USA: north, south, east, and west; the Great Lakes; the Midwest; the Rocky Mountains; Texas; Oregon; Florida; and California. You name it, we've lived there! It has been a roller coaster ride, and we are ready to leave this chapter behind. But first, after all these years, a significant party is called for.

On a snowy morning in Colorado, we sit in our kitchen and plan out a schedule of events. Then we prepare invitations for about fifty people to join us for a retirement party that we hope will be not just fun, but memorable.

Daughter and super-mom Heather does a superb job of designing and printing the invitations. They are tucked into wine glasses and placed in boxes, and within three days they are on their way to friends near and far. The guest list mirrors our life and the trail we have taken over the years. Since few of our friends can resist a good party, within a few days we have a guest list of thirty-six, all ready to celebrate this overdue retirement and to experience *la dolce far niente*—the sweetness of doing nothing—in the Umbrian countryside.

I return to Italy to make the preparations. I reserve the restaurants, choose the menus, select the wines, and negotiate the prices. Finding accommodations for this many people in and around Lubriano proves to be a major challenge.

The preparations proceed apace. I find that it's actually easy to plan a party in this part of the world, once you get past the language barrier. You can be absolutely certain that you are not going to get a bad meal, and you are not going to get bad wine either. Sunny weather, lovely scenery, and the atmosphere of the Italian countryside are provided free of charge. Having a party in such a far-off place is a great people filter. You won't have guests sitting at the table who would rather, say, be at a baseball game. All the people who come will have demonstrated that they really want to be there.

So let the party begin!

And then everything falls apart.

With really dreadful timing, I have a sudden health crisis. Just five days before the arrival of our guests, David has to rush me to a hospital in Rome. The ever-suave medical professor who attends me for the next five days tells me that he recommends major surgery—the sooner the better. I explain that this is simply not an option for me. I have thirty-six guests arriving from all over the world in a day or two for a party that I'm determined to host. Reluctantly, he releases me from the hospital about four hours before the arrival of our first guests. I weakly make my way back from my Roman hospital bed to Braccioforte, wondering how I'll ever be able to pull off the party we have planned for so long.

Daughter Heather completely takes over the reins, God bless her. Richard has ended his sabbatical year; he is back on his career track and living in New

York, hard at work. I miss him—no more cooking with Pierro and no more writing the great American novel. Our son Anthony and his wife Beth are here for the first time. He is an investment banker in Los Angeles, with a hectic bicoastal career.

Everything proceeds on schedule, the preparations continue, and the guests start to descend on Lubriano. The village is full of all these strangers—*Americani*, *Inglese*, and *Sud Africani*. In a little place that seldom sees a foreigner; they have never known anything like it, at least not since the Visigoths passed through here a few centuries ago. Anyone who looks vaguely American or English, even if they are not part of our party, is sent to our house by the locals.

As we expect, our guests are charmed by this Orvieto Classico region with its rolling hills dotted with vines, sunflowers, and sheep. Secure in the knowledge that they cannot fail to enjoy themselves, we challenge everyone to three days of eating, drinking, and generally luxuriating in the incomparable pleasures of *la dolce vita*.

The main event is held in the private dining room of the Monaldi palace, where not long ago we attended that incongruous pizza party. The Giordano family, as gracious as ever, has arranged everything for us. In this lovely, spacious room, under the gaze of the marble busts of three Caesars, the thirty-six of us sit down to a memorable dinner. In the best Italian fashion, course follows course, and rounds of wine are liberally pressed on us by our hosts. Our son Anthony makes a touching emotional speech toasting his fine dad and his long career. As we normally think of Anthony as a tough cookie, many of us are moved to tears by his heartfelt words. Friends follow with toasts of their own. We are delighted to have so many of our family and friends in one room, as though they have taken our jigsaw puzzle of a life and put all the pieces together.

Dancing follows the dinner, and there are more toasts in the ballroom. Then traditional Italian desserts appear, seemingly a different dessert for each person there: *Panna Cotta* (*recipe page 355), *Tiramisu* (*recipe page 351), and Almond *Tortas.* Glazed fruit tarts punctuate everything.

An impressive army of *grappas*, cognacs, and other, more mysterious Italian drinks are set out on a massive and ancient buffet, itself a work of art with its carved cherubs and curlicues. The evening is perfect, the dancing goes on. The frescos on the ceilings smile on us. They have looked down on many a feast, but to us it's all new—new and, even in spite of my health hiccup, terribly exciting.

26

SILVER WEDDING—ITALIAN STYLE

With David now in permanent residence and our construction schedule slowing down, our social life improves immeasurably. It is time for me to throw off my dusty, torn work clothes and partake of the town. David loves the Italian life—not the Italian builder life, but the walk-through-the-vineyards, three-hour-lunch kind of life. As Richard learned Italian in a heartbeat, David learns *la dolce far niente* with as much speed. The sweetness of doing nothing suits him well.

Today the Giordano family is once again extending us a warm invitation. They have invited us to celebrate their twenty-fifth wedding anniversary with them and their family. The palace is full of activity.

A couple of months prior to this event, we had a miscommunication with the Giordanos. They had invited us to the Palazzo to celebrate the first communion of their two youngest children. The huge celebration in the ballroom was already taking place when we arrived. It looked like a multigenerational football match. Giordano family members from all over Italy were running to greet each other, arms flying in welcome as young children wove their way in between huddles of kissing relatives. David and I were under the impression that our invitation was just for a drink before lunch, so we surreptitiously slipped out just as the meal was about to be served. Later that afternoon Gloria appeared at the back door with an extremely large plate of desserts and a message from Carmela saying she was sorry we couldn't stay for lunch. I sent back a thank-you note and a message saying we hadn't realized we had been invited for lunch, as we thought it was a family affair. The Giordanos were obviously not happy with our reply: Gloria appeared again, a week later, with a message saying that they hoped we were not upset with them because we didn't stay for lunch.

Damage control was obviously necessary. With flowers in hand, and a lot of translation help from Gloria, I communicated to the family that we were terribly sorry and that it was my lousy Italian; I had had no idea we had been invited for lunch too.

With this incident fresh in mind, Angelo very slowly and meticulously invites us to their twenty-fifth wedding anniversary celebration. He spells out in very rounded, slow Italian and in minute detail the entire proceedings of the affair soon to be celebrated. It is to be a church service, followed by lunch in the ballroom back at the Palazzo. He makes us repeat what we think he was saying. He is taking no chances.

On a lovely, chilly Saturday, the celebration starts with a church service at the little Rococo Madonna del Poggio church on the edge of town. It appears that everyone else was invited to be there at 1:30 p.m. but we have orders to be there at 1 p.m. (just in case, I suppose). We arrive and see no one there at all—it is just the warden and us. We nip into the bar across the road from the church, order a glass of wine, and watch for the arrival of the first guests. We are on our second glass of wine before the first very chic people begin to arrive.

A lovely royal blue carpet leads down the aisle and up to the altar. Two very grand velvet kneelers are in place for bridal couple. On the dot of 2 p.m., the whole congregation turns around to see Carmela and Angelo standing at the church doors to make their entrance. There is a loud fanfare of music. Carmela looks impossibly young. She always has that air of sophistication around her, even when wearing a scarf and an apron. She has the proud and at the same time friendly look of Sophia Loren. Angelo today is looking more like lord of the manor. The two slowly and solemnly make their way up the aisle.

That is, until they see us.

Angelo leaps into the pews and in a loud voice says, "Deeannah! You *do* remember you are invited for *lunch?*"

He then skips back into the aisle and resumes his stately procession up to the altar.

Very soon after the service ends, the congregation finds its way back to the palace. Soon another football huddle starts in the family ballroom. There is a huge pile of gifts at the entrance to the grand salon. I learn a very refreshing Italian custom: it's just fine to go ahead and open all the gifts that people bring you. You can do this immediately, even before the first guests are enjoying their aperitifs. Carmela and Angelo are falling on the pile of presents as though they are Visigoths sacking Rome. Paper and bows are flying and boxes are being ripped open. It's all unrestrained, pure joy as they race to give each present giver a huge hug and kiss, even if they are in the far flung corners of the ballroom. I like this custom. Boxes always beg me to rip them open.

Carmela and the palace staff have set a thirty-foot-long table in the middle of the ballroom. Course after course after course is brought on large silver platters from the kitchens.

Each time another course is delivered, everything is devoured immediately by a bevy of relatives. Teenagers are sitting with their arms wrapped lovingly around their *nonne*—grandmothers—and old men are standing in groups around the edge of the room in animated huddles. Angelo is keeping a sideways eye on us, making sure that we are not going to run away.

27

YOU DON'T BRING ME FLOWERS

Full many a flower is born to blush unseen,
And waste its sweetness on the desert air...
(Gray's Elegy*)*

When we arrive back in Lubriano after a winter in Denver, our garden is looking sad. Watering the garden is not Gloria's forte; it is marginally better than her housecleaning. It's all or nothing with her. In truth, I think that while we are gone she is more interested in sitting in the garden smoking cigarettes than watering flowers. She insists on giving the plants either no sustenance at all or what she calls "vitamins." The dose of "vitamins" comprises large overdoses of fertilizer, which send the shrubs into sudden death. My heart sinks when I see all the dried, dead plants that we lovingly planted the previous summer. All the while we were gone I have envisioned skipping into the garden of Braccioforte to be greeted by flowering roses and big rosemary and lavender bushes. No such luck—the scene is desolate.

Gloria says she is trying to save water, but our water bill for three months is hardly more than $40 a month. This is the epitome of false economy. Having planted copious shrubs and plants before I left, I find a sorry sight. Greeting me are parched sticks that look as though they have had a very long stay in the Sahara Desert.

I can now see that during this very short visit of just two weeks we will have to jumpstart and catch up with spring. My first order of damage control is to visit the little *Fioraio*—flower shop—in the neighboring town of Bagnoregio. It's a cheerful little store that has many different colorful plants sitting outside on the street. No Gloria lives here.

I park nearby, where four old men are supervising some road works. An old man in a really beat-up old red Fiat flags me down as I walk down the road. The words *"Piano, piano"*—quietly, quietly—filter out of the car.

He calls out, *"Ciao, bella!* (A common form of greeting, not too much should be read into it.) He tells me his wife has died and he is looking for company. I try my best to appear concerned about his plight and not offend him.

"I am very sorry," I tell him. "*Sono sposata*"—"I am married" —but going through my mind is: "The only occupant of a red car I'm going to run off with is the driver of a very well known fast red car with the rearing horse on the front."

I amble towards the *Fioraio* and start looking at the healthy, vibrant selection of plants for Gloria to kill. Not seeing any prices, I ask the man standing by a rosebush.

"What is the price of this and what was the price of that?" I shoot off questions at him. He goes to extraordinary lengths to find the price tags for me. He is very courteous and helpful. I then ask questions about compost. He speaks good English and is quite knowledgeable.

"I'll take six of those rose bushes and six bags of compost, and a few of those geraniums, too," I say to him. I ask him to wait for me to bring my car around. He obligingly waits and piles all of it in the back of my car.

As I walk into the store to pay, he doesn't follow. He gives me a smile and a wave and says, "*Ciao Signora*," and starts walking across the street.

"Hey!" I call out. "Don't you work here?"

"No," he says, laughing and waving at me again as he wanders off down the street.

Welcome to small-town Italy.

28

ALL THAT I KNOW

Each time I come back to our village I look at the old people passing me in the street. I wonder what stories they have to tell and how many years they have left in which to tell them. I think that these people are national treasures, yet they and no one else knows it. You can see it on their faces. To me, every one of these old souls is beautiful. Each wrinkle tells a story. There are no facelifts here to wash away the time and tides of their lives. There are stories, I am sure, of suffering, and also stories of love and laughter. The old men of this town were young men at the time of the World War II, and the old ladies I see limping painfully along the street would have been young girls. Who knows what privation they had to endure through those awful war years?

The townsfolk have told me that the village church steeple was hit in 1943, but there was no other damage. This lack of action was probably due to town's "backwater road to nowhere" status. On the other hand, Civita, across the valley, was not quite so lucky. With its fortress-like situation, the retreating Germans used it as a holdout, and the nearby town of Bagnoregio was a stronghold of partisan resistance. Today you can visit the Allied cemetery nearby and stand in sadness at the rows of crosses erected to all those young men who were killed as they pushed the Germans back up the Tiber Valley towards Florence and the Arno.

Walk through this cemetery, and you will see it was truly a World War. There, under the olive trees of Italy, lie buried some Zulu men from my hometown in Africa. I take a photo of the graves and send it back to the Zulu king, so he can know too.

There are many stories about World War II. Clateo, as always, is full of stories. We are sitting in the sun. He sits with his feet firmly on the ground and his hands lightly resting on his knees. He tells us that his parents were living with their young family in Rome during the war. There was no food in the city, so his father would take his bicycle and ride the eighty miles to his home near Lubriano. Ride eighty miles over narrow, dangerous roads, patrolled by Germans, eighty miles through the occupied countryside of the Lazio, over the passes and through the Sabine hills to

Lubriano. There he would load his bike with food and return to Rome. The rich countryside would give forth its bounty. His father would furtively walk the laden bike back to Rome on unpatrolled back roads and sometimes through fields, oftentimes through muddy farm fields.

The goal was simple—to avoid the German soldiers who would not hesitate to take everything from him: his provisions, his battered bicycle, and, with no compunction, his very life, if he resisted them. In this way he managed to feed his wife and children and also to keep a neighbor, a young widow with five small children, from starvation. The journey back to Rome would take him four days.

Clateo meanders on to another story. An American plane crashed in the Calanchi Valley, the same valley that we look onto from our house. The pilot, badly injured, was rescued by three young Lubrianese men. These men, two brothers and a friend sheltered the pilot in a hidden spot and nursed him back to health until he could be smuggled out. But there were spies everywhere in those times, and the Germans learned what had happened. Retribution was brutal, and all three were shot. Two of them died, but by some miracle one brother, though badly wounded, survived.

The pilot whom they'd saved returned to America and eventually recovered from his wounds. The war ended. The pilot returned to civilian life, and thirty years went by. But some debts cannot be forgotten, and the pilot knew that he had such a debt.

He knew he must go back to Italy and find the men who had saved him.

And so he went back, back to Lubriano, back to where he had nearly lost his life. It was an emotion-charged reunion. Until he arrived, thirty years later, he had not known that two of his saviors had paid for their heroism with their lives and only one was left.

As the wine flowed and all were swapping stories about where aunts, cousins, and nephews were today, a strange story emerged. It turned out that the pilot's wife, who was third-generation Italian/American, was a relative of his surviving savior.   Clateo is not as impressed as we are with the story. "You know these Italians, they used to have such big families, and everyone is related to everyone else anyway!" he says as he taps the table with his fingertips, then settles back to eat a fig.

☙❧

I ask Gloria to give me some help in recovering some tales from the old folk. Who are some of the *anziani*—the old ones, as the Italians call them—who might agree to sit down with me and tell their tales?

"Start with *Il Maestro*. He knows everything and everyone. He has old books, old pictures. Start with him."

Il Maestro is the long-retired school principal who has spent his entire working life at Lubriano's little school. He has devoted his life to the village and its history and children. She says he is the keeper of some very old record books about Lubriano. Why he has them and not City Hall I am not quite sure.

We invite the schoolmaster over to our house. He is a man of about eighty, still sprightly, even handsome. He looks fit and healthy for his age and walks past my window every day with a spring and a swagger in his step. He is upright and very well dressed, always in a suit and a hat. He comes in and I ask him how he is.

"Old and poor," he replies.

I invite him in to sit by the fire, as it's a bitterly cold day. He won't accept coffee or a piece of cake. No, he says, he never eats between meals. I offer him wine, but he says that in his whole life he has only drunk wine with meals. He could never accept a drink before and never after. Whatever else had gotten this man through life, it's obviously augmented with good habits.

He is very uncomfortable. At first he says that he doesn't want to be quoted on anything, and since his wife died a few years ago he doesn't want to have his photograph taken. It's not long, though, before he opens up and tells me the oral history of Lubriano. He says there are still Etruscan families living in the area. They have last names of Ollia, Herennia, Vettia, and Lorcia. He says there are even Etruscan tombs with crosses on them. This means that even though the Romans obliterated most of the Etruscans, some were living here well after the time of Christ.

He says that there are tombs in the cliffs right under our house. He says they are like a honeycomb. Of course the tombs have long since been raided and their funerary urns are sitting on some art collector's shelf. The tombs are on privately owned land, and the old schoolteacher says that we need to make an arrangement to see them. The only problem is that they're a little difficult to get to.

"It is *molto pericoloso*! We will have to go down by the means of a rope!"

In the year 1695 Lubriano was devastated by a large earthquake, and a whole part of the village slid into the valley below. The road that would have led to these tombs is now lying in rubble at the bottom of the valley.

We are amazed that an octogenarian would even think of rappelling down a cliff.

Il Maestro says he was drafted by the Fascists to serve in World War II. He didn't serve on the front, but was put to work to keep supply lines open. He says he was forced to sign up at the age of eighteen, just before the end of the war. He said it was common practice to sign up and then desert, which I gather was what he did.

He says he is of Roman roots, and judging by his nose, he is. He tells us that he has no cares in the world. Whenever something troubles him, he simply hands his cares to Saint Procolo. This is Lubriano's own personal patron saint, a shepherd who lived here in the fourteenth century. He miraculously healed a flock of sheep that had been slaughtered by wolves.

But it was another miracle witnessed by all in the local church that assured him of sainthood: he cured a young boy who was crippled and unable to walk. The boy's cane was thrown aside before the whole congregation. To this day it is enshrined in the village church. This humble symbol, the little cane, is depicted on the coat of arms of the village of Lubriano.

Il Maestro is sad that times have changed the village. None of the young people can be bothered to work the fields. In his day, he says, everyone worked the land, and everyone helped everyone else. He notes that the words for company and country are the same—*compagna*. This word itself means *con pane*—with bread. So company and country come from the word "with bread," and yet today people ignore the importance of the countryside, with its roots so intermingled with company and bread.

As he walks out of our front door he casually mentions the old record books he has somehow acquired. He adds that one day soon he will show them to me.

The next old man Gloria suggests I talk to is Romolo. He is one of the four men who occupy with amazing regularity the bench at the entrance to the village. He has big, black, sparkling eyes and the kind of looks that must have won all the girls when he was young. He is tall and upright. Signor Romolo walks in, hat in hand, like a farmer of old. He says he doesn't understand why I have invited him over to talk about Lubriano.

"But I'm not from Lubriano," he explains apologetically. "I only moved here in 1948!"

I suppress a smile, and ask politely, "Where did you come from, Romolo?"

"Civita," he answers, gesturing toward our neighboring village across the valley. As the crow flies, it is only half a mile away.

I suppress another smile. I guess it takes a while to get accepted around here.

The town of Civita is easily visible from our home, and if you shout loudly enough you can probably be heard across the valley. But Romolo doesn't identify with the Lubrianese. He tells me that they speak a different dialect in Civita.

He says that he fought for the Germans for one year. He fought at Frascati and at Cassino. He returned to his hometown of Civita, which the Germans used as a massive *magazzino*—a weapons storage center. His grandfather was killed in 1944 by the Americans, and his father was wounded. Thirty people, including his grandfather and his father, were holed up in a bunker in one of the cliffs under Civita. The bunker was hit by the Americans as part of the Allied push up through Italy to drive out the Germans.

Romolo said he could see that the Americans were approaching with heavy artillery, and decided that instead of hiding in the bunker halfway down the cliff-face, he would flee to a cave in the hilltop village itself. He guessed that on the highest point of the promontory he would be out of range of the Allied guns, and he was right. This move saved his life. But his eyes mist over as he describes how those who mistakenly sought refuge in the bunker below were killed when the Allied shells destroyed their bunker.

The Germans, in retreat, blew up the one and only bridge linking Civita with the world. It was only in the 1960s that this bridge was rebuilt with American money. A precariously small, dodgy foot bridge slung over the remains of the ancient bridge was what Romolo and all the inhabitants used from 1945 and into the 1960s.

But, he tells me again, he is lucky, because he was not sent to Russia. His good friend was. At the end of the war he walked all the way back from Russia to the Italian border. This man is nearly ninety now, Romolo tells me, and in very good health. I feel terribly wimpy.

Romolo then tells me that he is from a family of farmers. He married in 1955 and moved across the valley to live in Lubriano, his wife's hometown. I make a mental note of their wedding day and promise myself that I will not forget their fiftieth anniversary.

His wife, he says, had a good job as the cook for thirty years to the last Princess of the Monaldi, who is the last of her line and the former owner of the Giordanos' Palazzo. He tells me that his wife is eager to show me the special way that everyone in Lubriano cooks chicken. "It is from the *Principessa*, and the only correct way to cook chicken!" he says. It is called Chicken *Buione* (*recipe page 319)!

Romolo and his wife lived in the servants' quarters in the palazzo. Today they live in a small house across the street from the Palace, down a tiny pedestrian lane. He worked his whole life as a farm laborer and was paid on the ancient system of *mezzadria*. This is the Italian equivalent of sharecropping, where you don't own the land, but you farm it, then give half the crop to the land owner and keep the other half for yourself.

This *mezzadria* system, many believe, is what has kept many parts of Italy, especially south of Tuscany, embedded in poverty. After Hannibal routed the Roman army at Lake Trasimeno, many fled south, and large tracts of land were swept up by wealthy families, perpetuating a system of "winner take all" and assuring that peasants were kept in miserable conditions with no hope of ever extracting themselves from it.

I write on my calendar "Romolo and his wife— married for fifty years 10th Sept."

By chance we happen to arrive back here for the wonderful fall on exactly the tenth of September. It's good to be back. The figs are ripe for the picking, and there are warm smiles all around. I go right away to buy a bottle of champagne to take around to Romolo and his wife. Mass is being sung in the church across the square from their house. I wander down the little alley with my bottle of champagne. There is an old shrine sandwiched in between Romolo and his neighbor's house. It looks like a converted guardhouse. Who knows what it may have been for? It is right opposite the service gates into the palace. It's a shrine that looks almost Greek Orthodox, with a highly elaborate brass candleholder hanging from its diminutive roof. Bare wires run down the chain. Someone, now probably expired, must have gotten tired of replacing candles. As in all village shrines, there is evidence that a devoted person tends it from time to time. Flowers in varying degrees of freshness crowd in front of a miniature of the Virgin Mary.

I ring Romolo's door bell. There is no one home. Anticipating this, I have brought a card with me. I step four steps to the right, past the shrine, and ring a neighbor's doorbell. I recognize the man who answers. He is the one who always sits next to Romolo on the bench in the square.

I ask him, "Can you help me, Signore? What is the name of Romolo's wife?"

Blank stare and incredulous blank stare. More incredulous blank stare. I think he is blushing a little.

He looks at me.

He shrugs his shoulders and shouts into the house for his wife.

She comes to the door and looks at him in some exasperation. "Rosa," she says.

Well, I guess if you have lived next door to someone for just forty years, you really can't be expected to know his wife's first name.

The next day Gloria says that Romolo and Rosa are very touched by the gift of champagne, but they don't know who is this "Signora Armstrong of Via Roma 17?"

They come to Via Roma 17 to see who has given the champagne.

"*Molto gentile, Signora!* No one remembers us old people," says Rosa. "No one remembers."
Small favors, large rewards.

ॐ~ॐ

The day is chilly and I am walking down Main Street. Today there are no "four men on the bench" as the wind slices through town. A cat darts down an alley. There will be no street chats today. Just as I am wondering what all the normally endlessly chatty old people are doing with their day, a rather imposing and well conditioned smooth wooden arched double door opens up and there is Rosa, with a beam all over her face. She looks like the beginning of a story. She grabs my arm and pulls me inside.

"*Prenda un caffe?*"—would I like coffee?

I walk into a large room. The gentle hum of conversation stops. Twenty octogenarians look up from their cards and their coffee and everyone looks surprised. Some smile, some just look at me. Rosa leads me to the back of the hall. Under a muted mural, the oldest person in the room, a lady well into her nineties, stands next to a slick steel espresso machine.

"*Prenda un caffe?*" says the oldest barista in the world.

She has a row of demitasse cups neatly displayed in front of the machine, each on its own little tray. It is four o'clock in the afternoon, and I really don't need the caffeine. Even though Rosa will not let me pay, I see that the price is 50 cents. I wonder what the patrons at Starbucks would think about that. A few years ago, I was living on Sunset Boulevard in L.A., and every morning movie stars stood and waited to be served by young, arrogant baristas who thought they were God's gift to the fresh-roasted-coffee-starved public.

A group of about six gather at our table.

"I'm interested in hearing some stories about daily life in the war years," I say.

This comment is met with little or no response.

I think I must tread carefully, even after more than sixty years there may still be bitter feelings about sides taken. Today, they say, they would prefer to talk about the *Principessa* who owned the Palazzo Monaldi, the grandest building in town. It was very sad, another man told me, leaning on a cane. She died with almost nothing, in a small apartment nominally rented to her by dear Luigina of Lubriano's fruit and vegetable shop.

Back in the 1940s the Palazzo was the focal point of a working farm. The ballroom of today, where Stone Caravan recently rocked, was yesterday's *frantoio*—an olive mill. The olive oil was *ottimo*—the best—one lady with some missing teeth tells me. She says that her husband complained once that the olive oil was too expensive, and the *Principessa* didn't talk to him for twenty years. The *Principessa* had two daughters; she didn't like them and started selling all the land around here for nothing and ended up with no land and no income and a big place (I'll say) to keep up. She sold all the land and then the Palazzo for nothing. One lady tells me that they would have liked it very much if I had bought the palace. Another man with a hound's-tooth singlet and pocket watch tells me that the German commandant lived in the Palazzo during World War II, but he never evicted the *Principessa*.

"So here we are, they have segued themselves into the War," I think to myself.

Yes, the Germans were not so bad, and nothing much happened in Lubriano. This was the consensus of the group. There were big battles two miles away in Bagnoregio and ten miles away in Bolsena, but here there was not much excitement. All the Germans did was sit around all day and shoot at birds. They had lots of ammunition but no food.

"And they were as hungry as we were!" the oldest barista says. "We hid all our animals away deep in the forests, especially our pigs."

"Not in the Carbonara Forest, though," says the man in the singlet. "I was fourteen then" he says, "and the Germans paid me well. We stacked tank shells in the Carbonara Forest, so high that the mounds of shells nearly reached the tops of the trees. If one bomb had been dropped on that forest, our entire region would have been destroyed and everyone in it. When the war ended I took the money I had made, and bought my father two pigs and a cow. That was a fortune of wealth in those meager postwar days."

I feel emotions welling, good and bad, and I think it time to leave. When they were young, they didn't have anything—but they were young.

"*Arrivederla, Signora!*" They are being respectful by using the formal form of *Arrivederci.* "Please come back and we will tell you more, and make sure you come back on Thursday because on that day it is a church festival and that means the coffee is free."

29

FEASTS AND FESTIVALS

SPRING
Festa delle Donne

Today is the day of the *Festa delle Donne*—The Festival of the Ladies. This is a day for women to celebrate their womanhood. On this day all women in Italy honor their female family members, friends, and even acquaintances. This is a day where women all go out together, the day when ladies give each other a sprig of the beautiful mimosa bush.

The yellow bush is the first to flower at the very hint of spring. Its delicate little flowers are like glints of sunshine dotting the otherwise drab late winter landscape.

This festival takes me completely by surprise.

My neighbor Pasquina comes over with a lovely sprig of mimosa. She shoots words at me like a machine gun as she tries very hard to explain to me the concept of *Festa delle Donne*, but I'm not getting it. She rolls her eyes and sighs hugely at my lack of Italian vocabulary. I tell her "*lentamente*"—slowly. The first two words out of her mouth are a little slow, and then she revs up again to machine gun speed. Pasquina has a look of complete shock that I know nothing about *Festa delle Donne*. I feel like an Eskimo taking part in a Hawaiian luau. I can see her mental wheels spinning out of control.

Later that day, as I am visiting an antiques shop, the lady owner comes running out to the car to hand me a bunch of these soft blossoms.

That night Deutzia, the owner of Trattoria del Pozzo, gives me a sprig too. Her restaurant is filled with tables of women, all enjoying the night. The table next to us has about twelve women of all ages. Everything is very relaxed and we women are all smiling inside. Deutzia finishes off our menu with a Mimosa Cake (*recipe page 357). It is a light, airy sponge cake with lemon icing and cake finely crumbled on the top to look like the delicate bunches of mimosa that have been lovingly passed from woman to woman.

Lemons scent the air.

I tell a friend in Florida about this lovely day and she arranges a "Festival of the Ladies" at her church as a fundraiser. She says everyone comes—

great-grandmothers come with grandmothers who come with mothers who come with daughters. It is a veritable mitrochondrial chain. We need a day like this in the USA.

Sister to sister.

෬ඏ෯

La Infiorata

Spring is everywhere showing its colors, and in the midmorning sun the hilltop town of Civita di Bagnoregio beams at me from the valley, so close it's almost in front of my face. The church bell chimes the hour over there in Civita, always thirty seconds ahead of our Lubriano church.

Tomorrow is Sunday and the Feast of Our Lady of Lubriano, known among people in the area as *La Infiorata*. For the past 250 years, on the sixth Sunday after Easter, the residents of Lubriano have been celebrating this day by covering their one and only street with flower petals. On this Sunday every year the townfolk transform the charcoal-colored granite of the street into a dizzying artist's palette. Spring blossoms will decorate the paving for half a mile from the eleventh-century Church of San Giovanni Battista to the seventeenth-century Chapel of Santa Maria del Poggio. From year to year the priest and the people will come and go, but constancy will reign in *La Infiorata*. The colors of spring, like a river, flow through time.

We have never been here in May before, so we aren't quite sure what to expect. Signora Gaspari explains the rules. Tomorrow our two families will be responsible for entirely covering our sixty feet of road frontage with flower petals. Oh, yes, and they must all be freshly picked.

Easy for her to say. The Gasparis are one of the four big families in town. They can call in a small army of brothers, sisters, children, nieces, and cousins living in the general area as reinforcements to scour the surrounding hills and meadows for buds and blossoms. We, on the other hand, would have to call five different cities in the USA for a troop deployment of *la famiglia.*

Our daughter Heather is vacationing with us in Lubriano with her small children, a promising source of labor. Unfortunately she has picked this day to visit Florence. She is definitely in need of a break, but at least she will be back tomorrow. I try to interest David in the project, but he makes it pretty clear that his job description doesn't include anything having to do with flowers. So my tiny army of flower pickers consists of my ten- and eight-year-old grandsons and my five-year-old granddaughter. The boys are most enthusiastic and work diligently all day, but little Anna is more interested in climbing trees than picking blossoms. At lunchtime I pause to take stock of our progress, and realize with a sinking feeling that we have picked only a fraction of what we need. I know that our flowers are supposed to be picked by hand, but we just don't have enough hands. The solution is obvious. It's time to cheat!

I hasten through the village to the little garden shop, which is about to close. I hurriedly negotiate with the owner to buy all of her remaining flowers. There is no one else in the garden shop, but the Signora agrees. For a mere twenty Euro she will sell me armfuls of flowers that on Monday will be past their sell-by date. Included in this armful are about 150 Gerber daisies. The colors are stunning; half the basket load is coral and the other half is burgundy. My stress level down, I return to our blossom-filled back garden and fragrantly pluck away at apple blossoms, cherry blossoms, and garnet rose bushes. At dusk we are done—physically, that is. The petal scents turn the house into a perfume factory.

Pasquina has instructed us to meet in the street the next morning at 9:30 a.m., with our baskets of flowers. We will then chalk out our design onto the street pavers. At 10 a.m. the street will be closed to traffic and the laying of the flowers will begin. At 10:45 a.m. it is *molto importante* that all is done. At 11 a.m. sharp, the long religious procession will begin to walk barefoot over our artwork.

Angst keeps me awake all night. It seems an impossibility to strew that many flowers in that amount of space, in a complicated design, in that short a time. My only solace is that the street narrows exactly where our house is; at this point it is only nine feet wide. At 9:30 a.m., a cannon sounds in the valley below, obviously telling the community that the *festa* is ON! Even though the clouds are ominous, there appears to be no rain delay.

I start by chalking my part of the street. Being no artist, I again cheat. With the aid of a broomstick and the children's jump rope, I mark out giant circles. The neighbors look quite mystified by my makeshift compass. My anxiety disappears when a contingent of seven Gasparis appears with huge laundry baskets full of petals of cherry pink, sunshine yellow, and magenta red. Pasquina is *la maestra* and conducts the concerto of flower flingers. She has chalked the word "love" in the center of our display, which I think cute and kind, given that she speaks no English at all. We all work like crazy for forty-five minutes in floral harmony. We begin by thinly spreading the petals on the road, not knowing how many flowers it takes to cover sixty feet by nine feet of cobbles. Like children coloring with crayons, we stand back, admire, then go back for more color and accentuate all the borders with green leaves to form a frame. Blossoms of pink, yellow, white, and magenta and deep red rose petals are all iridescent in the ominous light of a possible thunderstorm. I top off the designs with my Gerber daisies, which, despite their origins, are gratefully received.

The whole town now feverishly sets out to see the full effect of how, in just one hour, an army of homeowners can transform a town. We all quickly side step down the edge of the street to assess how others have fared florally and artistically. Everyone is being very careful not to step on anyone else's petals. For as far as I can see, up and down our street, the four-hundred-year-old houses look happy. On this one day each year they reside along the banks of a river of flowers. The color of it all meanders with the curve of the street, babbling away into the distance.

Large concentric circles, drawn with or without a broomstick, dot the stream of flowers. Some villagers have written their initials with spring's proliferating sunny *ginestra*—broom—and then there is the occasional big white cross of small downy petals. In front of the fruit and vegetable shop "*Ave*" is spelled out in velvety red roses. Luigina, the owner, lost her father last week.

Angelo Giordano in his palace has the longest street frontage. There he is, standing proudly in front of his palace doors, which anyone in Beverly Hills would kill for. He is looking unusually well rested, just like my husband. He hugs two of his six daughters and poses proudly in front of his 120 foot flower fest. I am sure his family and staff feel just as frazzled as I do.

I wander past the palace down Main Street towards the bar. The people at this point in the street have also cheated. The effect is pretty impressive. They have dyed fine wood shavings all sorts of bright colors; just as we used flowers, they have used wood shavings. They have created a very intricate portrait of Our Lady of Lubriano, the Madonna del Poggio herself. I would like to think this dust is from the workshop of Lubriano's one and only cabinetmaker, who under no circumstances will work with any wood but chestnut.

Pasquina whispers to me, "*Piu bella*"—more lovely. We all nod furiously. The town's monochromatic medieval cobbles are now bursting with color and fragrant scents, and everyone has a spring in their step.

At 11a.m. I sprint up to my bedroom and noisily call to my daughter in the next room, "Where is the iron?" We have been invited to a First Communion celebration immediately after the procession ends. Still amazed by the speed of it all, I peek out of my window to check that I'm not dreaming. I'm startled to see the priest silently standing below me with all the procession formed behind him. The procession is so long I can't see the end of it. The people are so still they look like an Italian version of the Terracotta Warriors. Everyone is waiting for the band to signal the start of the parade. I feel like a noisy buffoon acting up in the middle of a minute of silence.

Solemnly, a trumpet sounds somewhere behind Don Luigi. He steps forward and slowly, like a train leaving the station, the procession glides forward. Right behind the priest, the church's icon is held up high by three young ladies. They're followed by an armada of barefoot celebrants. The first few devotees are young girls covered from head to toe in black garments, their faces hidden as if in mourning; their black-stockinged feet accentuate the brilliance of the petals underfoot. They're carrying gigantic white altar candles that are as tall as they are. Gloria gives me the scoop. These young women, she tells me, are young ladies who owe a great debt to the Madonna and are humbling themselves in fervent thanks for prayers answered. The enormous candles they're carrying are the altar candles for the coming year.

Everyone in the procession looks quite polished. The village garb of butcher's apron, baker's hat, or shoemaker's leathers are all put aside for today. Our Italian teacher, Emilio, is right behind the priest, looking very solemn in shining white robes as he holds a big wooden cross up high. Our garden contractor, Roberto, is flanked by two small girls in pink satin robes who look like a couple of Raphael's cherubs, which I am sure they're not. Two marching bands follow the procession. The second band is a very smart contingent. They all have massive iridescent black feathers fluttering atop their helmets, bobbing to the beat of their step like an army of rooster tails.

The procession passes on our petals. At first I wince a little as our design is scuffed, but the crushed, scattered flowers waft still more perfume into the air. Our floral canvas is losing form and turning into a misty Monet as it is deconstructed before our eyes. In five minutes our design is gone. Looking at the flowers all mixed up, I wonder which is better—before or after? The new potpourri at my feet is a testament to nature's glory, all pearly white, cherry pink, sunshine yellow, burgundy, garnet, and coral. The new palette mocks me. To think I believed I could make a better design than spring itself!

Fifteen minutes after the procession has disappeared, husbands, including mine, bring out just-emptied laundry baskets and old boxes. With great gusto the street is swept clean of every last petal. I see the mayor, dressed in his suit for Mass, sweeping too.

The sweet, sweet blossoms' hour is past. Father Don Luigi is saying Mass, and the heavens open up with a good soaking rain.

SUMMER
The Feast of St. Procolo

Summer is a time to put everything aside; it's time to sit around our giant round terracotta table at the bottom of the garden. We are shaded by our beautiful old fig tree; I lean back and pick a fig. Pasquina tells me that I must eat the fig within one minute of picking it off the tree, with the milk still seeping from the stem; that way it is the sweetest. Pasquina would never put up with the slow supply line of produce that victimizes American shoppers. I can just imagine her going into my supermarket in Denver and asking for a just-picked fig.

"Should I come back later for a fresh-picked one?" she might ask, as she already asks Luigina in the local fruit and vegetable shop.

Breakfast starts with the arrival of a just-baked loaf still wafting up its aroma.

"*Pane con sale*," my friend calls out as a breakfast bell.

We have a summer morning ritual at Braccioforte. We pick figs off the tree and eat them immediately with local honey and *pecorino*. We buy the local soft, sweet sheep's milk cheese at the Monday

222

farmers' market in Bagnoregio. There is a saying in Italy: "No one knows cheese like a Sardinian shepherd." Our favorite local *pecorino* is smooth, sweet, and at the same time tangy. It is produced by a Sardinian ex-shepherd who has a farm just outside Lubriano with 1,200 sheep.

∂∾∾ఄ

Summer is a time for taking it easy. Construction is put aside; many houseguests come and go, and talk of Michelangelo (apologies to T. S. Eliot).

∂∾∾ఄ

In late summer Lubriano celebrates the Feast of Saint Procolo. This patron saint of Lubriano was first mentioned to me by Il Maestro, the old school teacher. The saint has the honor of having his skull paraded through the town once a year. Granted, his head is encased in a rather magnificent gold filigree reliquary, but given the right light you can catch a rather gruesome glimpse of Saint Procolo. There is much excitement here on the saint's day. There is a marching band. All the little old men are dressed up in their funeral suits. Today they don their dashing hats and ties too. The parade begins around noon. Everything is very solemn. Everyone puts their hands behind their backs and bows their heads as the reliquary is paraded by on a bier carried on the shoulders of four church elders.

On the same day as the Feast of St. Procolo, there is a feast going on in Civita di Bagnoregio across the valley. I can hear a band warming up over there. As there is a great rivalry between the towns, I wonder if each town has chosen this feast day to annoy the other. The feast in Civita is a *palio*—a medieval horse race—but not like the grand horse race in Siena. Civita races donkeys. David and I appear to be the only people who have it in mind to attend both festivals. No one in Lubriano seems the slightest bit concerned that there is a festival going on in Civita and vice versa. The only reason we know there is a *palio* in Civita is because of Rick Steve's *Guide*.

We arrive in Civita, racing, puffing, up the footbridge. We think too late, but in fact just in time for the first of the donkey trials. A smart young man is roping off the arena with some police tape. We recognize him as the young waiter of about fourteen who seems to run a whole restaurant in Bagnoregio. He always seats us, takes our order, and adds up our bill. He operates the computerized cash register too. He looks very official today in a starched white shirt and black pants, the same outfit he wears when waiting tables. I imagine he plays Frank Sinatra rather than rap music on his iPod. The mini piazza in the middle of the town is merry with three rows of people skirting the entire piazza waiting for the event. We have it in mind to have lunch here today, but all three restaurants are closed. It appears that nobody has worked out that this is the biggest tourist day of the year. I suppose all three restaurant owners are riding donkeys.

As part of the pregame show, a rather skimpy brass band is creating a din—the trumpet is being played by our plumber, who breaks away from the band and serenades me for ten seconds with "Hello Dolly." Surrounding people are as amused by his little jog out of line as am I. About three hundred people are waiting for the race to begin—two hundred and ninety more people than you ever find in Civita.

The first donkeys are ushered onto the course, but no one and nothing can budge them. One look at the crowd, and the donkeys have their sights set on leaving the piazza—definitely not running the required four laps around the piazza. It appears that the young waiter is also a jockey; in fact, he wins his trials and then also the final race. His donkey is as professional as he is, and is quite superior to the other donkeys, which look quite scruffy and are just as disorganized as their riders. After about an hour, David and I decide that if we are taking bets in life, we should put them on this young man.

FALL
Festa Castagne e Vino

In late October, when the weather turns rainy and cold in Umbria and the Lazio and all the feasts and festivals are over, one last festival appears on the billboards at the edge of town. It is the chestnut festival. I'm surprised to note that it's to take place right in front of our house. Seeing that there is no space in front of our house, I am a little startled. There is, though, one narrow pedestrian lane that drops off Via Roma and descends into the valley. It services the houses that cling to the cliffs in front of us. The name of the road is *Vicolo Scenditoio*—"small descending road." This is an understatement. How anyone can think of having a *festa*—feast—here I have no idea. They must have exhausted all other locations and possibilities.

The weather, as predicted, is misty and rainy, but we are leaving to go back to the USA the next day so opt to go anyway. We arrive an hour early due to the fact that we have no television and no paper in our Italian home and have therefore completely missed the end of Daylight Savings the day before. We only discover our time change error the next day when the taxi driver shows up an hour late to pick us up for our flight back to the USA. By the time he arrives, we are in a fury about missing our flight. After a very difficult explanation about the time change in rudimentary Italian, we eventually get it and feel quite stupid.

Our arrival an hour early at the Chestnut Festival is quite fortuitous, as the management committee running the feast is in the process of canceling the event. In true Italian tradition, they welcome us with gusto. We are brought into the fold of organizers. In a tiny little courtyard no more than twelve feet by twelve feet, they have an open pit fire. Firewood is glowing. The fire is built directly on the stone cobbles with a few stone blocks stopping the fire from spilling over onto the nearby houses. A giant triangular rig about ten feet high sits over the fire, with a four-foot-wide barbecue rack suspended about three feet above the fire. As we arrive the men throw a few bucketfuls of chestnuts onto the rack over the fire. With a lot of enthusiasm they shake the barbecue rack continuously from side to side as they perfectly roast the chestnuts.

While this is going on, the rain is really starting to pour down. One of the nearby residents invites us into his cellar to await the arrival of the roasted chestnuts. His cellar runs right underneath Via Roma, and he tells us his cellar was built in the twelfth century. One wall is actually from the year 1000 AD and forms a foundation wall of the present church. Winemaking equipment at least a century old is strewn everywhere. After about fifteen minutes, the chestnuts are brought into the cellar, served in brown paper cones. The aroma reminds me of New York in the winter—and here I am, light years away from New York.

The secret to eating chestnuts Lubriano style is to dip some raisin bread into red wine and eat it along with some roasted chestnut. It's pleasingly full-bodied and substantial on this rainy night. We go home in the pouring rain with arms full of roasted chestnuts. We get the fire going in our kitchen and continue the Festa in the warmth of Braccioforte.

In retrospect, we feel lucky that our Daylight Savings error led us to be the only participants in the *Festa Castagne e Vino.*

୬ଡ଼ଡ଼ୄ

Festival of the Mushrooms

Gloria appears on my back doorstep to announce that there is a mushroom festival in a little town called Sipicciano. This little village, she says, is not far across the valley, about a thirty minutes' drive away from us. This village does not appear on any map I own. Beautiful color posters show velvety tan and auburn mushrooms, all enticingly displayed on copper. The posters are all over town. Gloria says the town is near Graffignano and is only about a fifteen-mile drive down the Tiber Valley.

We have friends staying with us. They are anxious to taste the famous porcini mushrooms of our area which are available for a very short season in October and November.

We mark the date on the calendar. On a rainy Saturday afternoon I put a cut of veal (* recipe page 339) in the oven to roast slowly while we are gone. I prepare it in the Lubriano way: browning it on top of the stove in olive oil, butter, and garlic and then transferring it into a heavy casserole. I add a little wine and place it in the oven. We will bring back plenty of mushrooms to serve with this veal roast. We set off with three friends from the USA for the Festival of Funghi.

We wander down through Castiglione in Teverina, through beautiful rolling countryside, and stop at the stunning winery of La Madonna della Macchie to have our attitudes adjusted. We come to Graffignano. It is one of the ancient towns in the Tiber Valley—nothing grand like Orvieto or Cortona, but just another of the many little towns in this area built up high to get away from the marauding hordes of the many centuries past, whether it be Goths, Visigoths, Romans, Charlemagne, or Hannibal—you name them. Conquering peoples who all tried hard to subdue this valley on their journey to the big prize of Rome.

After various stops asking locals where the mushroom festival is and receiving many puzzled looks, we eventually see Sipicciano, which appears to be a village of about five hundred. It is perched on the edge of the Tiber Valley, right on the border of Umbria and the Lazio. Like an ancient eagle, it looks down from its aerie onto vineyards and olive groves and over in the far distance towards all the traffic speeding between Rome and Florence.

We had not seen a single sign for a Mushroom Festival since we left Lubriano. What we find here is a village surrounded by fortified walls. Unlike its neighbor Orvieto, nothing has been restored. There is not a soul in sight. Eventually we come upon a church and happen to notice a few people scurrying to the back carrying baskets. We follow.

What we find is a hall behind the church. Locals arrive with baskets at the back door of the church hall and are greeted by a very official man with a mushroom reference book. He picks up their mushrooms in his gloved hand and analyzes them. It soon becomes clear that this is a festival about mushrooms NOT to eat. Here we are, with raging appetites for *Funghi* with Lasagna, *Funghi* with Polenta, *Funghi* with *Vitello* and *Funghi* with *Bistecca*, and we find ourselves at a festival of inedible mushrooms.

The display is quite incredible. There are mushrooms that will kill you, mushrooms that will give you hallucinations, and mushrooms that are merely toxic. There is not a fat porcini mushroom amongst the whole lot. They are categorized and displayed for all to see. From the display of about a hundred and fifty mushroom varieties there are only about ten that are edible. A good rule of thumb is don't go out picking mushrooms because they will probably kill you, give you hallucinations, or, at the very least, make you sick.

After being chastised by this very sobering display of toxins, we set off back home. I vow to season the veal roast that is at this point simmering in my oven with something other than mushrooms. The roast will be sad, as it is waiting for the final garnish of porcini that would have been garnered from the Funghi Festival.

On our way home, we decide to return to Castiglione in Teverina and to the local winery Madonna della Macchie in order to save the day. The owners are a little surprised to see us back so soon. They greet us with a bottle in each hand filled with their Orvieto Classico – a cheery, slightly fruity white wine. They also see we look hungry and bring out a lovely wheel of local soft Umbrian *pecorino* cheese.

Feeling a little consoled, we drive back to Lubriano. My friend suggests that we go to Luigina's fruit and vegetable shop on the off chance she has edible mushrooms. After viewing the display at the mushroom festival, I think this is a very brave remark.

I envision us and our guests all expiring around the fire after our meal.

As we walk into Luigina's shop, what greets us is a gift from heaven. In a basket right by the door is a mushroom of such grand proportions it is astounding. There is just one mushroom for sale. It is about one foot in diameter. "*Fragrante*," says Luigina. We smell it, and are all sold on this one mushroom that actually weighs four pounds. She says they call it "mouse ears" in Lubriano, as it resembles about one hundred mouse ears all clumped together. The main thing going through our minds at this point is that it looks absolutely nothing like anything we have seen at the anti-mushroom festival. We buy it.

Half an hour later our dinner is ready with its mushroom topping. I cut the giant mushroom into one-inch cubes and sauté it in olive oil, garlic, and butter. I then add porcini mushroom stock and let it simmer until the stock has completely evaporated. I let the chopped mushrooms crisp up to a toasty brown. And then, at the final moment before serving, I add some cream, it is delicious and we fall in love mushrooms all over again.

30

TO FALL IN FALL

That time of year thou may'st in me behold,
When yellow leaves, or none, or few do hang.
(William Shakespeare)

Dinner is again on my mind on this chilly September afternoon. We have spent a lovely afternoon in the area around Montecchio, in the beautiful hills that overlook the ink-blue waters of Lago Corbara. We sit having coffees in the picture-perfect town square that strains to look over the Tiber Valley, soaking up as much of the sun as we can. A little alley looks charming, filled with pots of cascading geraniums from every available balcony. The little street is full of rusty-colored houses built of *tufa* rock; ancient, broken-down doorways; and iron railings all rusted through.

"Psst, psst!" beckons a strange voice. A tired and unkempt man beckons us to come up the alley as though he were an illegal trader wanting us to see a knockoff purse or pair of sunglasses.

This rather stressed-looking man jabs his index finger towards the back of his station wagon. I stand back and David walks forward, not wanting to look and at the same time unable to help himself. This is not New York City, and the chance of getting two tourists per day in Montecchio, let alone in this alley, is highly unlikely.

The jittery salesman flings open the trunk to reveal about thirty wheels of aged cheese. He produces a strange-looking object from his pocket, like an apple corer for baby apples. In no time at all, he is plunging it into one of the cheese wheels and drawing out a sample for us. It is an Umbrian *pecorino*, quite soft and very sweet, not like its cousin Pecorino Romano, which tends to be hard and dry. He has a farm nearby, the salesman tells us, and he sells his cheeses out of the back of his car.

The cheese is heavenly. It is soft and creamy as velvet, but at the same time just a little spicy. We buy a whole wheel. He speeds off, having made his sale for the day, and we speed off in search of some good wine to accompany our cheese.

September is a gentle time of year. It's the time of the *vendemmia*—the wine harvest. The light is soft, and a little mist from the cool evening air has settled into the folds of the valley. Grape pickers sit between the vines, enjoying the break from their work, and we are all enjoying the glorious Italian final harvest of grapes, fire-engine-red tomatoes, and arugula as green as Ireland. It is hard to believe danger is lurking around the corner.

Just as the sun is setting we arrive at the winery Madonna della Macchie, about a ten minutes' drive from our house.

"I'll run in," I say, "and see if the place is still open."

A sign on the gatepost shows that olive oil and wine are for sale. I step inside the gate and start to call "*Ciao, Ciao!*" to attract attention, as it appears that no one is around. The gate is open, so I walk in, hoping to find someone and be served.

All of a sudden, in the low afternoon sunlight, I see a huge German shepherd stalking me.

"OK, don't panic," I think to myself, remembering an encounter with an old elephant a couple of months ago while visiting Africa. The words of the game guard pass through my mind: "Back up slowly and don't turn around and run. Just back up slowly."

I back up, but the dog keeps coming.

"OK, don't panic yet. This dog is on a leash, and I'm standing a couple of feet inside the entrance. I'm definitely out of range," I think to myself.

At first I do not realize, as the dog keeps on coming, that its leash is not attached to an immovable source but rather to an overhead guy wire. It suddenly dawns on me that I'm standing well within the dog's range. I think, as if in a dream, that I'm a target in a police training video. The dog leaps up and lunges at me. I put my arm up to protect my face as huge teeth grab at my arm to bring me down to the ground. My silky jacket saves me; I feel the dog's teeth slip off my arm and rip into my jacket.

I feel myself jet propelled backward by the dog and land with my feet just a few inches out of the range of the dog. The guy wire ran out. My arm is broken by the force of being propelled backwards by the dog. I think I might have rather taken the advice of another African game ranger when we saw a herd of African buffalo:

"Agh! Man! Buffalo! Don't wait around to see what a buffalo is going to do, just run like hell as fast as your legs will take you."

I should have treated this dog as a buffalo and not as an elephant.

The rest of the afternoon is a blur. If you have the choice, break your arm in the USA, where you will be treated by kind, gentle doctors and nurses. In Italy, where healthcare is free, you get what you pay for. My arm is stretched and set in a heavy plaster cast without my even receiving a painkiller. It's hard to see any humor in this situation. The pain is excruciating for a month. David tries to humor me on our various follow-up visits back to the Orvieto hospital by making up rhyming songs to the tune of the old Italian song "Amapola" because the doctor's name is Dr. Amendola.

"Dr. Amendola,
Someone hit me with a roller,
And now my arm is *rotta* (broken),
Help me, pleeease.

Dr Amendola,
A dog bit me on the shoulder,
And now my arm is *rotta*
Set it, pleeeease."
Etc., etc.

The owner of the vineyard is beside himself. He is terribly upset. He is so sorry he left his gate open. He should not have done it, he says. He is not the patrician kind of vineyard owner whose picture you see in an advertisement for Italian wine. He is short, portly, boasts a huge, mousy, long beard, wears denim overalls and great big hobnail boots, and has hands brown with the Umbrian earth. He follows us in his car to the hospital. He threatens to bury the dog alive as he storms around and around the emergency area in between trying to get me to drink some coffee. It makes me realize that the American legal system has really shut people up; you never, ever get to hear anyone in the USA say they're sorry. If Madonna della Macchie Winery had been located in California, I would have been awarded quite a settlement and be sitting on the winery's porch, directing the wine harvest operations and inviting people like Robert Mondavi to come and visit me.

Alas, my Italian settlement was out of court. We accepted a large supply of olive oil, a few cases of Orvieto Classico for our new cantina, and a written promise from him not to harm the dog, for it was not the dog that left the gate open.

31

UN GATTINO STUPENDO

One of the saddest parts of village life is seeing the way Italians treat their animals, in particular cats. Lubriano has turned out to be both literally and figuratively "a four-cat town," as Gloria pointed out our first week here. Often there are four cats sitting on or near the piazza. They are at best tolerated. I am sure they keep any mice problem at bay. It is obvious that in the Italian mind, cats have no value except as rodent hunters.

Each year a new crop of cats hangs around the village, and by the next spring they have all disappeared, the victims of starvation, foxes, and poison put out by farmers. That is the outflow. The inflow comes from a most unusual source. Several people have told us that when Italians take their vacations, usually in August, the sad reality is that no one wants to be bothered with arranging to feed a pet for that vacation month. Besides, everyone takes their vacations at the same time. As a result, thousands of cats, and dogs too, are abandoned along freeways. For an animal lover, it's heart-wrenching.

We are always in a Catch-22 situation. Feed one cat at the back door and a cat-call goes out all over town that the Signora is back in town and food is available. Pasquina has made it very clear that she likes me a lot, but not my cat fetish.

Not long after the dog attacked me in the vineyard, I am sitting feeling sorry for myself in the kitchen. Gloria bursts in the back door with some whiskers peeking out from between her fingers and a muffled wail coming from her fist. The noise reminds me of the call of a distressed bird. Unbelievably, in her palm is the smallest kitten I think I have ever seen.

"Signora, that bad boy who thinks he is the Mayor of Lubriano, at age eight, has a lemonade stand today"—which I had seen—"and he is selling kittens"—which I had not seen. He sold two and now this one he can't sell, and he is going to throw it in the valley, so please can you help?"

Apparently three small, motherless kittens had been found at the cemetery. The self-appointed Mayor of Lubriano had seen a business opportunity.

Gloria brings the kitten in for fear that Signora Gaspari, who sees through walls, will send the kitten to the same place she sends bunnies.

I have a weak idea.

We often see a mother cat that miraculously, at whatever time of year, has two kittens in tow. She is the only cat in this "four-cat town" that seems to survive the harsh reality of being a cat in Italy.

"That cat is not a cat, she is a rabbit!" says a neighbor.

This cat has taken up residence in the vacant garden attached to ours. We call her Nebbia, which means "fog" in Italian, for she is a beautiful misty grey and has gentle, soft blue eyes.

"Perhaps Nebbia will adopt this kitten!" I tell Gloria hopefully.

We walk out into the garden to locate Nebbia, who is not indisposed to accepting leftovers from us and our house guests. We put the kitten down close to where she normally sits. Her two kittens of the moment appear to be about four weeks older than this little midget of a thing. The midget squawks, which quickly brings Nebbia onto the scene. The kitten snuggles up to Nebbia and begins suckling...for ten seconds, that is.

All of a sudden Nebbia raises her paw and, with a giant *WHACK*, brings it down on the kitten's head. She leaps out of the way in horror.

Things are not looking good. My arm is broken, and in four weeks we are leaving to go home to the USA. There is simply no possibility of keeping a tiny kitten here in Lubriano.

"You must tell the boy we can't help him with this kitten!" I tell Gloria.

She leaves with the kitten.

Ten minutes later she is back, still holding the kitten.

"Signora, I promise you, that boy is cruel, and he is going to throw it in the valley below. His mother will not let him bring a cat inside their house."

And so the story of Micio in our life commences.

I have no idea what to do with a kitten that is still blind and cannot even lap milk. I empty my contact saline solution bottle out and turn it into a diminutive feeding bottle. David and I take turns getting up to feed this little creature in the middle of the night. He is completely in love with this ball of fluff. He plays Andrea Bocelli music in the middle of the night to soothe himself and the kitten. We call him Micio, which is not very creative, as it just means "kitten" in Italian. He is very demanding, and with incredible speed he learns to climb up our clothing and latch onto our ears as a replacement for his mother.

We are completely in his clutches.

I now commence trying to find Micio a home. I visit local pet shops. Apparently pet shops in Italy do not deal in kittens. Tarantulas, hamsters, snakes, and birds, yes, but cats, no. I gate-crash a veterinarians' convention in Orvieto and ask an astonished group of vets, "What can be done with a stray cat?" There is no shelter for cats. They simply shrug their shoulders.

Cats appear on no one's radar here.

Deutzia, our restaurant owner/friend who is the one recognized cat-mad lady in the community, has a dozen cats living behind the trattoria. But this is more than she can handle. She tells me that one day a few weeks ago in the mid-afternoon, when the restaurant was closed, she saw the priest mysteriously driving away from the restaurant parking lot. Her dogs began barking wildly and she went to investigate. There in the parking area were three little kittens. The priest is obviously much smarter than I—of course Deutzia took them in.

After two weeks of night feeds and constant harping to the village people about the need to find a home for this dear kitten, we realize that our chances are slim.

Micio has a huge personality, and we are captivated by his "You will take care of me no matter what" attitude.

Heather, our dear, kind daughter in the USA, offers Micio a home. She now has three young children, a new baby, and two cats, but she offers Micio a home. Kind and loving Heather will not go to rodeos, as she cries at the calf roping.

This is a most generous gesture, but how will we get the kitten to her? We are sailing home to the USA, and I hardly think Royal Caribbean will accept a cat in our cabin.

We start finding out how to ship a cat to the USA because we have exhausted all Italian adoption possibilities.

My broken arm is killing me, and I am taking a stray cat that I do not want in the first place to the Orvieto vet so that he can receive shots, a microchip, and yes, an Italian passport complete with photo? We also have paperwork to fill out that is incredibly complicated.

In our crazed state we have bought Micio an airline ticket that requires all of the above.

The airline tells us they won't accept a kitten under three months old, so we lie, saying he was malnourished and therefore looks younger.

We drive Micio to Rome at 3 a.m. before we board our ship for Miami. We get lost at the cargo facility at Rome Airport. We are sitting in the car with the sun rising over Rome and Micio is sitting on David's shoulder, biting his neck. We appear to have gone stark raving mad.

There is a tap on the window. "*Signore?* Are you the people shipping a cat to Florida?"

"Well, actually, I often sit here in the middle of the night at the Rome Airport cargo facility with a kitten sitting on my shoulder!" replies my husband sarcastically.

"That kitten is very small for three months," they tell us as we hand him over to the airline attendants in Rome.

All this while, Micio has not a care in the world. He has his inspection before boarding the flight and causes a stir at the cargo office by pouncing on the computer keyboard of the ticketing agent and biting his fingers.

"*Un gattino stupendo*" is the consensus of the airline staff.

All the while a very special, highly pedigreed Persian cat who is to be shipped alongside Micio is receiving no attention at all.

So Micio the immigrant is carried away by smiling airline attendants. He has gone. His dreams and his fears are to be American ones.

"I wish I could get a green card, too," says Gloria.

"That is one lucky cat."

32

JUST WHEN YOU THOUGHT YOU WERE OUT OF THE WOODS

As if breaking my arm isn't bad enough, to finish the year off, just as we are thinking we have a habitable residence we have two new matters to deal with.

One very stormy, chilly evening we look up at the fresco in the *salone* and find that water is pouring from our lady's bellybutton. During our first week back in Italy for the fall, we had been having trickles of water down the wall in the living room and had sent an alarm phone call to the owner of the apartment above us, who lives in Rome. But this is more than a trickle—it is serious. We pull the terracotta-and-glass coffee table out of the way and find really bad mold growing on our antique kilim rug. This adds to our strong suspicions that Gloria has lost interest in us and no cleaning whatsoever has taken place in our house since we have last been here.

David finds a workman who has a key to the apartment above. We stumble through the doorway and are confronted with piles of damp rubble and some wonderful old furniture crumbling under spiderwebs. Every surface is covered with a thick layer of dust. The place looks as though it was subjected to either a raid by the Germans in World War II or a drug raid in some decade past. We pick our way through the reception rooms to get to the offending room that is leaking water right through into our house.

What we are not expecting when we look up is to see daylight. Several tiles are missing. In fact, the roof over our heads is useless, and our neighbor's floor is all that lies between us and the elements. The deed of sale for our house states that the roof to our house is jointly owned by us and these people, so this is half our problem.

We think back to the beginning of our remodel, when Gregorio was trying to persuade us to buy his brand new townhouse, and wonder if we should have listened.

All our contacts in town need to be marshaled. Agostino is definitely off my wish list, and Mario is completely entrenched at the palace. Our Italian is improving, and we decide to branch out on our own and circumvent Gloria's Italian-English dialect and her contacts. We will go forward on our own without a translator and find different workmen.

The house in front of ours is being restored by a young man who looks as though he has been to Scotland and bought one of those joke plaid berets with a scruffy wig sticking out from under it. But the hair is his. Nazareno is his name. He is always on the job, all day and every day, something that has rarely occurred when doing our remodel. We invite Nazareno over to look at the problem; he is horrified. It is quite disconcerting when a local Lubrianese who has seen it all feels we have disaster resting over our heads.

Nazareno calls in his cousin from Civita to help with the crisis. He is a dapper man with a little moustache, and his hat is made out of an old cement bag that he has fashioned into a type of sailor's hat. If these two men came to my front door in Denver, I'm not sure whether I would laugh or run away. But here and now, it is time to keep them. David does a sterling job of marshalling the money from the neighbor for his half of the payment for the new roof *before* the job has begun. Judging by the state of the place above, things may be a little tight for these neighbors.

The street is so narrow that it's impossible to put scaffolding up on our house, so with typical Lubrianese village ingenuity they bash holes into our neighbor's living room's two-foot-thick walls and extend large logs out of our lovely old façade. They in essence build an overhanging balcony from which they can work. Our roof tiles are historic. The good ones have to remain, stored during work and then returned to the new roof. When all is complete, nothing will have changed except that Our Lady of the Fresco will have a dry bellybutton.

It's time to go home to Denver to enjoy our eleven-year-old house and its watertight roof.

The second matter to be dealt with doesn't come as too much of a surprise.

We see the writing on the wall when it comes to our employment of Gloria and Mario. Gloria has become dissatisfied with all things Lubrianese. Her attitude is descending; her cleaning and lawn watering have reached an all-time low. I think she wants to move on—out of Lubriano, and if she could, out of Italy. Cleaning our home, in spite of the good pay, has dropped off her priority list, and the shutters we gave Mario to refinish nine months ago are still in their sad state, propped up in the corner of their living room. Gloria announces that she will work for us when we are in the USA, but she can't work for us when we are in Lubriano. For a very intelligent human being, I'm not sure how she thinks we are going to fall for this one.

In the months we have been gone, Braccioforte has been given short shrift. And it shows.

Something will have to be done. We are sad, as she has been a great crutch and a never-ending source of information, amusement, and translation. But with our construction schedule winding down and a long list of houseguests on our calendar, we can no longer turn a blind eye to her shoddy housecleaning and plant extermination techniques.

We walk very carefully as we look around to replace Gloria, who has a huge ego. In Africa they say, "Slowly, slowly *catchee* monkey," and so we cautiously start putting out word around town that we need new help. We tell Gloria and Mario that we can see they're stressed, and that we can manage things just fine on our own. We pay them off generously so as to not burn Lubriano bridges. We let things settle for a few months before looking around.

Clateo, our ombudsman and consumer watchdog par excellence, takes over our keys. He is visibly delighted that we are letting Gloria go. His cleaning lady will clean a little for us while we are gone. We'll let sleeping dogs lie.

33

A NEW BROOM SWEEPS CLEAN

We return in spring to find a new world in Lubriano. Clateo is our savior; he has found an Albanian lady to work for us. He is secretly pleased, as his dislike for Gloria has grown; he has frequently witnessed her taking advantage of us.

Enter pretty, fair Nadia who looks rather like a 1950s housewife. She looks a bit like Meryl Streep's character in *The Bridges of Madison County*, standing there in her light cotton floral dress with her apron on. She is in her late thirties and misses her mother in Albania terribly; she cries when she talks about her.

Heather is visiting again from Florida with her brood of four children. Our son-in-law Seth is here too, to complete our family. We are delighted to be able to have all the family present. The children are the focus of the entire community. They are dodging *nonnas'* kisses as they walk home down Via Roma, and baby Tommy, with his white-blonde hair and sparkling blue eyes, holds court in a town full of dark, olive-skinned babies. Tommy is known through the town as *il nepotino biondo*—the little blonde grandbaby.

Nadia cannot stop hugging him. Even though both Nadia and Heather speak bad Italian, they have long, garbled conversations and shriek with a laughter that knows no language boundaries. Both of them are loving, dedicated people with a warmth of character that is captivating.

We have to improve our Italian to communicate with Nadia. We have been relying on the crutch that Gloria spoke excellent English. David is sure that I will now speak Italian with an Albanian accent, since I am forced to converse in Italian with a new Albanian immigrant. My irregular verbs, which were already bad, become worse, and Giuseppina, the butcher, asks why my Italian is not as good this year as it was last year. I am blasting through Italian, butchering it, and David is meticulously learning every irregular verb.

I buy an Albanian/English dictionary, but we soon throw it away and start talking in our pidgin Italian. Nadia has two children, both of whom look like the children of aristocrats from Milan. The ten-year-old girl, Aferdita, is often standing in the street on the chance that we may walk by. She has pen and paper in hand, and she is always ready for an English lesson.

She is like a dogged reporter, trailing us as we walk to our car. She and her brother were both top of their class within three months of arriving in Italy, despite the fact that they spoke no Italian upon arrival.

Nadia's husband is a builder, and is only too happy to be our handyman.

Within two days Nadia discovers the months of neglect our house has sustained, even as I walk down Lubriano's main street and smile sweetly at Gloria. Nadia seems less forgiving about the whole matter. Who knows how long we will have her with us, but we'll take her as long as she wants the work.

We really come from different sides of the planet, both literally and figuratively. Albania is one of the poorest and most backward nations on earth, America the richest. And here we are, on middle ground in Italy.

When we bought Braccioforte, I made a commitment to light candles for dinner every single night, to remember family and friends, to slow things down, and to give thanks for these years that some never get to see. In the evening, as the sun sets, I usually light about six candles in the kitchen. Nadia is not impressed.

"No, I don't like these candles at all," she tells me. "That is all we had in Albania. You should rather use the electric lights."

34

COVER-UP

Every time I cook in my Lubriano kitchen, my stance has me looking into my well. How lucky I am to be able to stare down a medieval well while I am cooking! I wish the pace of life in Lubriano had not got to me quite so entirely. The rush of discovery has gone, and I am now willing to wonder what is down there rather than dig.

A peace descends, as I am sure it has upon all the occupants of this kitchen before me, and I wait for things to come to me rather than go out and find them.

The pottery finds we have made are brought into focus by passive inaction rather than action.

The church of San Giovanni Battista, one hundred yards away from us, is a simple, restrained church. Everyone in Lubriano would tell you that it is quite old, but they are not sure how old. Not that anyone seems to really care in an area that was once the Etruscan homeland.

In 2005, after having been away for some time, we arrive in the town square to find the church all boarded up, closed for business, shut away from prayers. It appears that while repairing the church floor, the workers noticed bones... and some inscriptions long covered over by a repair after the earthquake in 1695.

History is not much of a subject for debate in Lubriano today. Quite a few villagers are miffed.

"What is this priest doing, digging up the old floor when it was perfectly fine—and now we are without a church?"

"Now we have to have all the authorities involved with all those bones they found. Why can't they just cover them up?" The general opinion seems to be "let sleeping dogs lie; this is all just a lot of nonsense."

My interest in the church is piqued, but in Roman Catholic Italy I am not sure that piqued *Protestanti* are too welcome. I am encouraged, though: after four years of our living here, Don Luigi, the local priest, last spring actually stretched his hand through my car window and shook mine. Then, in the fall, we exchange a few words in the town square. And now today, here he is, Don Luigi, standing in my courtyard, inviting me to come into the very much closed-up church, which is off limits to the public.

As the workers start to repair the floor of the church, what appears is a Christian Longobard Tomb from about the seventh century. This tomb is located under the high altar of the present day church. I am now standing at the dug-up altar, staring down into the eye sockets of a Longobard skull. I bless the fact that we have only found broken pottery so far in our partially excavated well.

The Longobards or Long Beards were a Germanic tribe and part of what is called in Italy "the Barbarian Invasion." These people moved into Italy in about 568 A.D. and established their kingdom, with its headquarters in what today is Lombardy in Northern Italy. In the sixth and seventh century, small factions broke away and there was, among others, a headquarters established in Spoleto, about a hundred miles away from Lubriano.

Don Luigi says that the authorities in the regional capital Viterbo came and took most of the relics to Viterbo. Nothing valuable, he says.

Don Luigi also tells me that the present-day Palazzo was from ancient times a convent, which was the center of a large religious community. His church was called "The Church of the Convent," he says. The fact that Lubriano was once a large religious center is corroborated by my visit to the Vatican Museum.

In the stunning maproom of the Vatican, Lubriano, which on this day has only eight hundred occupants, was the only town shown in this entire area on a sixteenth-century map, suggesting that Lubriano was an important church center at the time. Larger centers such as Orvieto are not shown on this map.

I start to research, trying to find out if ceramics were perhaps manufactured by this religious community, and I hit pay dirt. It appears that our area was known in the sixteenth century as a center for the manufacture of medicinal pottery. What we have in our well is a pile of broken rejects.

In Lubriano, all this is sort of ho-hum, and there is an air of aggravation rather than excitement about the whole thing. Just imagine if we found a burial site of such antiquity under a church floor in the USA? We would have TV crews from around the country covering the subject. But in Italy, this is apparently everyday business.

"When can we have our church back?" is the call of the community. "Can't they just cover that thing up?"

Everyone seems happy when the Vatican orders sand to be placed over this ancient burial site and the old terracotta tile floor to be replaced. Well, at least it isn't concrete.

I go home and look down my well, where we have dug through about one third of the dirt. David and I look at each other and decide this will be a very good project for our children and grandchildren. Covering things with sand for a later generation suddenly seems like an excellent idea.

We walk into the back garden, pick a few figs, sit at the terracotta table, and open a bottle of

Chapter 34

Brunello. We hear and see the church bell tolling the sunset in, and we are happy to toast the donation of a most unusual inheritance.

RECIPES

Recipes

Antipasti and Salads

Arugula Salad with Fennel, Spinach, and Parmesan
Salad of Finely Shaved Fennel Root, Fennel Fronds, and
    Apples
Richard's *Tamburi Neri*
Grilled Porcini Mushrooms
Tuscan *Panzanella*
Insalata Caprese
Diana's Rabbit Liver Pâté with Mushrooms, Cognac,
    and Garlic

Soups and Sides

Giuseppe's Tuscan *Carabaccia*
Braccioforte Fragrant Vegetable Soup
Braccioforte Breakfast *Frittata*

Primi

Umbrian *Pappardelle al Cinghiale*
Pappardelle con Funghi e Tartufi alla Diana
Richard's *Fettucine Tartufata* with Butter and
    Parmesan
Penne al'Arrabiata (Spicy Penne with Chilies and
    Parsley)
Linguine Semplice with Thyme and Pinenuts
Gloria's Lasagna with Porcini Mushrooms and Sausage

Pierro's Toasted Polenta with Mushrooms, Rosemary, and Sausage

Pasta e Fagioli

Tuscan Beans "*Fiasco*" (cooked over a fire in a wine flask)

La Badia Risotto with Radicchio and Cream

Secondi

Gamberi all' Piazza San Giovanni Battista

Bolsena's Sauteed *Corregone*

Signora Gaspari's $6,000 Rabbit

Lubriano Chicken *Buione*

Herbed Chicken with Lemon and Garlic

Hearth-Roasted Quail Stuffed with Rosemary and Garlic

Roast Goose with Caramelized Onions

Grilled Sausage with Rosemary, Onion, and Garlic

Roast Pork Casserole with Orvieto Classico Wine, Fennel, and Red Peppers

Giuseppina's Spit-Roasted *Porchetta* with Fennel and Sage

Giuseppina's Loin of Pork Roast with Sage

Bistecca Fiorentina

Slow-Roasted Veal Cooked with Wine, with a Topping of Crispy Mushrooms

Scallopine di Vitello alla Griglia

Vegetables

Spicy Roast Vegetables from Bagnoregio
Rosemary Roasted Potatoes
Slow-Roasted Onions Topped with Breadcrumbs
Diana's Fresh Herb Mixture

Dolce

Anthony's Grilled Fresh Figs
Gelato di Crema
Tiramisu
Cecily's Pavlova with Mixed Wild Berries and Cream
Panna Cotta with Fresh Figs
Festa delle *Donne* Mimosa Cake with *Limoncello*

෨ↄ෨

Notes

Arugula Salad with Fennel, Spinach, and Parmesan

The fresh arugula in Italy has more bite to it than the American kind! Adding the baby spinach to this salad enhances the flavor.

4 servings

Salad:
4 cups washed and cleaned arugula
1 fennel bulb, finely sliced
2 cups baby spinach
Shaved Parmesan (be generous)

Salad Dressing:
4 tablespoons olive oil
1 tablespoon lemon juice
1 teaspoon sugar
1 clove garlic
1 teaspoon Dijon mustard
Salt and pepper

Blend the olive oil, lemon juice, sugar, garlic, mustard, salt, and pepper and chill well. Toss the dressing into the greens just before serving. Shave fresh Parmesan generously on top.

❧❧

Notes

Salad of Finely Shaved Fennel Root, Fennel Fronds, and Apples

If you have a mandolin in your kitchen, use it for delightfully thin slices.

2 servings

1 fennel bulb, sliced extremely finely
2 tablespoons finely chopped fennel fronds
1 red apple, skin on, sliced finely
¼ cup olive oil
2 tablespoons lemon juice
Salt and white pepper

Toss all the ingredients together and serve on chilled plates directly from the refrigerator.

❧❧

Notes

Grilled Porcini Mushrooms

Porcini mushrooms (meaning "little pigs") are a very expensive, short-lived specialty of the countryside around Lubriano, especially available in the fall after a good soaking rain. No mushroom degrades more quickly than a porcini, so it is imperative to buy top-quality just-picked specimens. Porcini mushrooms become slimy in less than 24 hours so are difficult to get to market. If fresh porcinis are not available, try this recipe with the more accessible portabella mushroom.

4 servings

4 large porcinis or portabellas (stalks removed and reserved—freeze for use in a soup)
¼ cup olive oil
Salt and pepper

Heat a very heavy pan on top of the stove and bring it to an exceptionally high heat. In the meanwhile, clean the mushrooms well with a soft brush (do not wash). Brush the mushrooms with olive oil and sprinkle with salt and pepper.

When the pan is smoking hot, add the mushrooms and press down hard with a spatula so that they almost burn (two minutes). Turn over for one minute, press down hard again, and serve immediately.

❧❧

Notes

Richard's *Antipasto Tamburi Neri* – "Black" Zucchini Drums

You'll need a long pair of kitchen tongs for this, or a long barbecue fork, as the oil can spatter quite a bit.

8 appetizer servings

4 medium zucchini, sliced
½ to 1 cup olive oil (depending on the size of your pan)
Salt and freshly ground black pepper

Slice the zucchini into sections approximately as long as the zucchini is wide. (For a zucchini 2" thick, the slices would be 2" long).

In your widest pan, heat about a half inch of olive oil until smoking. Fry the zucchini in batches, standing the chunks on end, until both ends of each chunk are black. Do not worry about draining them; just put them on a platter and tent loosely with foil.

Season with salt and pepper, and serve *tepida* (at room temperature) with other antipasti.

☙❧

Notes

Insalata Caprese

Insalata Caprese *means "salad in the style of Capri." It is a test for tomatoes and* mozzarella di bufala *(which is made from milk of a water buffalo). There is no room for tasteless tomatoes to hide—the excellence of the final dish is very definitely in direct proportion to the superiority of the ingredients!*

4 servings

4 tomatoes, very ripe and sweet, sliced
Salt and pepper
4 ounces *mozzarella di bufala*, sliced
10 or 12 basil leaves, thinly sliced
Top-quality extra virgin olive oil
Lemon juice

Season the tomatoes if necessary with salt and pepper. Place on a platter, alternating the tomatoes, mozzarella, and basil. Chill until ready to serve. Drizzle with an excellent olive oil just before serving. If desired, add lemon juice. This salad should be served ice cold. If you have time, chill the plates too!

꙰

Notes

꙰

Tuscan *Panzanella*

This dish should be made 24 hours in advance.

8 servings

6 slices of good Italian bread, the staler the better
4 very ripe tomatoes, chopped into small cubes
1 small red onion, finely chopped
1 cucumber, peeled, seeded, and diced
3 stalks celery, finely sliced
1 teaspoon crushed garlic
10 basil leaves, finely sliced
½ cup olive oil
½ cup tomato juice
¼ cup red wine vinegar
Salt and pepper to taste

Served with:
6 cups mixed salad greens tossed in a very small
amount of Italian salad dressing

Cube the bread into ½-inch cubes, leaving the crusts
on. Set aside. Combine the remaining ingredients and
set in a low, flat glass dish in the refrigerator for 24
hours. Cover tightly. One hour before serving, toss in
the bread cubes. Season again to taste. Chill until
ready for use. Just before serving, spoon the *Panzanella*
on a bed of mixed salad greens.

⤜⤛

Notes

Giuseppe's Tuscan *Carabaccia*

This is onion soup, Tuscan-style. My friends tell me that Catherine de Medici took this recipe to France; today's French onion soup is derived from this dish and not vice versa, as the French would have you think!

8 servings

2 pounds sweet red onions, sliced
1 cup good olive oil (divided)
2 cloves garlic, crushed
1 carrot, sliced
1 stalk celery, sliced
1 large bunch basil, shredded
2 cups fresh or frozen green peas
½ cup dry white wine
6 cups strong chicken or vegetable broth
Salt and pepper
Tabasco to taste
8 slices toasted stale Italian bread
8 eggs
Grated Parmesan or Pecorino Romano cheese
Parsley for garnish

In a heavy ovenproof casserole, heat half the olive oil and add the onion and garlic. Simmer until the onions are limp but not brown. Turn the oven to 325°F. Add the carrot, celery, basil, peas, wine, and broth and bring to a boil. Season to taste with salt, pepper and Tabasco. Cover and place in the oven for 2 hours. Adjust seasoning.

Place the toast in the bottom of 8 individual ovenproof soup bowls and drizzle each with olive oil. Break an egg onto the bread and carefully spoon over the soup. Sprinkle with some grated Parmesan cheese and place in a 375^{0}F oven for about ten minutes or until the soup begins to sizzle around the edge. Garnish with parsley and serve immediately.

Braccioforte Fragrant Vegetable Soup

*In fall and winter I make up big batches of this soup.
We sit around the fire and eat bowls and bowls of it. If
there is any left the next day, I add fettuccine noodles
or small white beans to turn it into a one-dish dinner.*

6 servings

¼ cup olive oil
¼ cup butter
2 onions or 2 leeks, chopped
6 cups of chopped mixed vegetables such as carrots,
celery, zucchini, peas
1 cup chopped spinach
2 tablespoons Diana's Fresh Herb Mixture (* recipe
　　page 287)
One can (12 ounces) chopped tomatoes
8 to 10 cups of stock (beef, chicken, or porcini)
Salt and pepper
Tabasco
6 slices stale bread, drizzled with olive oil and toasted
　　in the oven
1 cup chopped fresh parsley
¾ cup grated Parmesan
Olive oil for garnish

Heat the olive oil and butter and sauté the onions until
tender. Add the chopped mixed vegetables, spinach,
Diana's Fresh Herb Mixture, tomatoes and stock.
Season to taste with salt, pepper and Tabasco. Simmer

covered for 2 hours. In the meanwhile, prepare the toast.

Take 4 cups of the vegetable soup and puree and return to the pot. Adjust seasoning. Add the chopped parsley just before serving.

Serve in 6 big soup bowls: place the toast in the bottom and add a tablespoon of Parmesan, then ladle the soup on top. Drizzle the soup with olive oil and pass the Parmesan around.

Diana's Fresh Herb Mixture

This mixture has a million different uses. It's a great thing to make at the end of summer. You can leave in some of smaller stalks of herbs too, as long as they are not tough or woody. Use this mix to enhance soups and stews or baste over grilled meats or vegetables.

Makes 3 cups of herb paste

5 cups fresh herbs such as basil, thyme, oregano, sage, and parsley (or any other fresh herb in your garden)
1 cup excellent olive oil
½ cup lemon juice
6 cloves garlic
1 tablespoon sugar
1 teaspoon salt
¼ teaspoon Tabasco

Roughly chop all the herbs together and place in a blender. (It is fine to leave a few very tender stalks, too, as they will be blended.) Add the remaining ingredients and blend until you have a fine paste.

Keeps in the refrigerator for 30 days, or you can freeze in a zippered plastic storage bag. Lay the bag flat in the freezer so that you end up with a thin slab of herbs, which is easy to break off a piece from as you would a piece from a chocolate bar.

∂∞∂

Notes

∂∞∂

Braccioforte Breakfast *Frittata*

This is my standard Braccioforte breakfast when we are entertaining casts of thousands! Make it all the night before and store overnight in the refrigerator. Leaving the frittata *overnight is important, as the bread takes on a soufflé-like appearance.*

8 servings

10 slices very stale bread, broken into 1" cubes
1 cup leftover grilled vegetables (optional)
2 large tomatoes, chopped, or one 12 ounce can chopped tomatoes
¼ cup pancetta or cooked bacon
½ cup chopped fresh herbs (oregano, basil, or sage)
8 eggs whisked with a fork with 3/4 cup milk
Salt and pepper
½ cup grated Parmesan cheese

In a deep, flat glass or ceramic dish, place the bread, vegetables, tomatoes, pancetta, and herbs. Whisk the eggs with the milk and season well. Pour this mixture over the bread. Cover and refrigerate overnight.

One hour before serving, sprinkle with Parmesan cheese and place the dish in a 250°F oven for 30 minutes. Increase heat to 325°F for 15 minutes or until the eggs are set.

Notes

Diana's Rabbit Liver Pâté with Mushrooms, Cognac, and Garlic

Rabbits have large livers relative to the size of their bodies. The liver from one rabbit will make enough pâté for about 10 people.

Makes 1 cup

1 rabbit liver, chopped, or 4 ounces chicken livers
1 small onion, chopped
1 clove garlic
¼ cup chopped mushrooms
¼ cup *pancetta* or bacon
¼ cup butter
¼ cup finely chopped sage
3 tablespoons good cognac
¼ cup chicken broth
Salt and pepper

Cook the onion, garlic, mushrooms and bacon in butter until the onion is tender. Add the chopped rabbit liver and sage and sauté for about 5 minutes. Add the cognac and continue cooking for 3 minutes. Season to taste. Add the chicken broth. Transfer to a blender and blend for at least 3 minutes until very, very smooth. Store covered in the refrigerator or frozen in the freezer. Serve on *crostini* - toasted white Italian bread.

❧❧

Notes

Umbrian *Pappardelle al Cinghiale* – Pasta with Wild Boar Sauce

Of all the things that I love to eat in Umbria, this is possibly my favorite. It's evocative of the mood of Umbria in the fall and winter. It's simple and flavorful, but it's not rich—just like the atmosphere here. The aroma of a wild boar sauce wafting from the kitchen brings back happy memories of kind Giuseppe. We enjoyed many lunches at Vecchio Mulino, often craning to get a glimpse of the spectacular valley view as seen by the chef in the kitchen.

In the USA ground buffalo is a good substitute for wild boar meat. Pappardelle are very thin, wide ribbons of pasta widely used in Lubriano. The best substitute is fettucine. The sauce is best simmered all day. It resembles a stew with pasta added!!

6 servings

12 ounces pappardelle

Sauce:
2 tablespoons good olive oil
2 tablespoons butter
1 pound ground wild boar meat or lean ground buffalo
    meat
1 onion, very finely chopped
2 tablespoons finely chopped celery

½ cup chopped lean bacon
2 cups good red wine
½ cup chopped tomatoes
1 tablespoon sugar
1 sprig rosemary
Salt and pepper

Heat the oil and butter in a heavy pan. Gently sauté together with ground meat, onion, celery, and bacon until the mixture is brown and all the juices have evaporated. Add the red wine, tomatoes, sugar, rosemary, salt, and pepper. Simmer gently, covered, at 250°F for 4 to 5 hours. Remove any fat before serving. The sauce may be thickened, if necessary, with a little flour and water.

Cook the pasta and spoon the *Cinghiale* Sauce on top just before serving.

Giuseppe, old friend, thanks for the recipe!

Umbrian *Pappardelle* with Fresh Shaved Truffles

This is a rare treat. Like mushrooms, fresh truffles are difficult to bring to market, as they lose their fragrance and pungency in a short amount of time. Also, in the USA, because of the high cost of importing, it is hard to know what a truffle tastes like because you wind up with such a meager shaving on your plate!

4 servings

12 ounces *pappardelle* or *fettucine* (cooked with salt
    per package instructions)
¼ cup melted butter
1 black truffle at least the size of a large grape
Salt and pepper

With a very soft brush, dust off the truffle. Do not wash.

Just the minute before serving, toss the pasta with butter. Season very well with salt and pepper and shave the truffle onto the individual plates at the table.

Notes

Pappardelle con Funghi e Tartufi alla Diana

Pappardelle *are noodles typical of Umbria. They are very wide, thin, flat ribbons of pasta, often served with porcini mushrooms, which are found abundantly in our area in the fall. This dish is ultra-simple and fragrant! If you want to make a showy splash, shave a truffle on top just before serving.*

6 servings

12 ounces dry *pappardelle* or *tagliatelle* noodles
¼ cup olive oil
¼ cup butter
5 cups chopped mixed mushrooms, preferably including some porcini
½ cup chopped *pancetta* or lean bacon
10 fresh sage leaves, sliced finely
Salt and pepper to taste
A few truffle shavings (the amount depends on where you are and how deep your pockets are!)

Cook the pasta per package directions. While the pasta is cooking, heat the olive oil and butter in a wide, heavy pan. Add the pancetta and the sage leaves. Cook lightly for 3 minutes. Now turn up the heat, add the mushrooms all at one time, season and cook. Keep turning the mushrooms so that none burn but all are crispy brown. Just before serving, fold into the cooked pasta. Shave the truffles onto the pasta at the dinner table.

～～

Notes

Richard's *Fettucine Tartufata* with Butter and Parmesan

Tartufata is readily available in Italy. It's a paste made of truffles and porcini mushrooms, and it's heavenly. It can be found in gourmet supermarkets in the USA.

6 servings

12 ounces *fettucine*
2 chicken or vegetable bouillon cubes
2 tablespoons *tartufata* paste
¼ cup butter
1 cup grated Parmesan
Salt and white pepper to taste

Boil the *fettucine* with the bouillon cubes instead of salt. Drain. Add the remaining ingredients. Season to taste. Serve immediately.

❧❧

Notes

❧❧

Pasta e Fagioli

This is a universally well-liked recipe, pleasing every age group. The flavor jumps right out at you.

8 servings

½ cup chopped *pancetta* or cooked bacon
¼ cup olive oil
2 onions, chopped
3 carrots, chopped
1½ cups fresh parsley, divided into 1 cup and ½ cup
½ cup Diana's Fresh Herb Mixture (*recipe page 285)
4 tomatoes, chopped, or one 12-ounce can chopped
    tomatoes
Two 16-ounce cans cooked cannellini or navy beans
1 large sprig rosemary
3 cups chicken or vegetable broth
8 ounces any type pasta, such as *linguine*, snapped
    into finger-length pieces
Salt and pepper
1 cup fresh basil, sliced into slivers
Garnish, if desired, with grated Parmesan cheese

In a large stock pot, sauté the *pancetta* in olive oil and then add the onions, carrots, 1 cup parsley, and herb mixture. Cook until the vegetables are wilted. Add the tomatoes, beans, rosemary, and vegetable broth, and season to taste. Simmer for 10 minutes. In the meanwhile, cook the pasta per package instructions, drain, and add to the bean mixture. Sprinkle with basil and the remaining ½ cup parsley and serve immediately. If desired, serve with grated Parmesan cheese.

Penne al'Arrabiata –
Spicy Penne with Chilies and Parsley

The name translates as "angry pasta." Note the absence of tomato in this recipe.

6 servings

12 ounces penne, cooked in lightly salted water
¼ cup high-quality extra virgin olive oil
3 small red hot chilies, chopped finely
1 cup flat-leaf parsley
5 cloves of garlic, crushed
Salt, pepper and finely ground red pepper
Lemon juice to taste

Heat the olive oil. Add the chilies, parsley, and garlic cloves to the pan and sauté gently until the garlic is completely soft. (It's a good idea to make this a few hours beforehand so that the chilies' heat can dissipate into the mixture.) Reheat before serving and toss into the cooked pasta. Season to taste with salt, red pepper, and if necessary, a little lemon juice.

၈၀၆

Notes

Linguine Semplice with Thyme and Pine Nuts

6 servings

12 ounces *linguine*
4 tablespoons olive oil
3 cloves garlic, crushed
3 sprigs fresh thyme
¼ cup pine nuts
Salt and freshly ground pepper

Cook the *linguine* as per package instructions. While the *linguine* is cooking, heat a saucepan and add the olive oil, garlic and thyme and lastly the pine nuts. Cook very gently until pine nuts are a honey brown, and then toss the linguine into the mixture. Remove the thyme stalks. Season to taste and serve with salt and lots of freshly ground black pepper.

Notes

Gloria's Lasagna with Porcini Mushrooms and Sausage

If you are in Italy, use porcini mushroom bouillon cubes. Unfortunately, they are only available in the USA in Italian food markets.

8 servings

Filling:
One 9-ounce package lasagna noodles
5 cups mixed mushrooms (preferably with porcinis included)
¼ cup butter
1 pound Italian sausage meat
1 tablespoon of chopped fresh rosemary
1 teaspoon ground dried thyme

Sauce:
¼ cup butter
2 tablespoons flour
2 cups half and half
1 cup milk
1 porcini or chicken bouillon cube
White pepper
3 large eggs

1 cup grated Parmesan cheese

Cook the lasagna according to the package

instructions. Sauté the mushrooms in the butter until brown and crisp. Cook the sausage with rosemary. Add the thyme. Prepare the sauce, melt the butter, and add the flour off the heat. Add the half and half and milk all at once and return to the heat. Stir over a gentle heat until cooked and thickened. Remove from the heat. Add the bouillon cube and stir in. Cool slightly. Now add the eggs to the sauce. Mix well. Layer the lasagna with the mushrooms and sausage, finishing off with the sauce. Now sprinkle with the Parmesan and bake slowly in a 325^{0}F oven for 45 minutes. If necessary, brown a little on top before serving.

Pierro's Toasted Polenta with Mushroom, Rosemary, and Sausage Sauce

8 servings

One 10-ounce box polenta, mixed according to package
   instructions
4 Italian sausages, skins removed and crumbled
2 sprigs rosemary
2 cups mixed mushrooms, chopped
1 cup milk
Salt and white pepper

Make the polenta according to package instructions. Spoon out the mush and press onto a greased cookie sheet. Cover with waxed paper and then cover with another cookie sheet. Place two weights, (such as a can of soup) on top. Place in the refrigerator for about two hours. Now remove weights, second cookie sheet, and paper and place under the broiler until polenta becomes a toasty brown color. Cut into squares and triangles.

In the meanwhile, make the sauce. Sauté the sausages, rosemary, and mushrooms. Add the milk and thicken if necessary with a little flour mixed with water. Season to taste. Simmer gently for about 20 minutes. When cooked, if desired, thicken the sauce with a little flour mixed with cold milk.

Somewhere South of Tuscany

To serve, place a slice of toasted polenta on a plate
and top liberally with the sauce.

Fagioli al Fiasco –
Tuscan Beans Cooked in the Fire in a Wine Flask

This is an old peasant dish. Beans are cooked nestling in the dying embers of an open hearth.

4 servings

2 cups hot water
1 cup dried white beans (preferably cannellini beans)
4 cloves garlic
8 fresh sage leaves
¾ teaspoon salt
1 dash Tabasco
¼ cup olive oil

Pour hot water into a wide-rimmed Chianti wine flask (750ml). Gradually add the beans to the flask and then the remaining ingredients. Cover the top with foil. While still warm, place the flask in the fire, in dying embers rather than in a roaring fire. Turn the flask a couple of times during the first 10 minutes so that the flask won't crack. Beans will take about 8 hours to cook. (Water should never boil in the flask; if it does, move a little further from the heat of the fire.)

This recipe can also be somewhat duplicated by cooking in a 250^0F oven for 5 hours.

∂∞∂

Notes

∂∞∂

La Badia Risotto with Radicchio and Cream

*When I asked the chef at La Badia Hotel if they could
tell me what ingredients were in this dish, he told me
"radicchio and cream"! Here is my version. Risotto
simply must be tender, and it does not wait well.*

6 servings

1 cup whipping cream
1 cup very finely sliced radicchio
2 tablespoons olive oil
2 tablespoons butter
1 small onion, chopped finely
1 cup Arborio rice
3 – 4 cups chicken broth
½ cup grated Parmesan
Salt and white pepper

Over extremely low heat, set the cream and radicchio
to gently come to a simmer. Cook very gently, covered,
while preparing the risotto, for about 20 minutes.

In a heavy, large pan, over a medium heat, heat the
olive oil and the butter. When butter is melted, add
the onions and softly sauté for 4 minutes. Add the
rice. Reduce the heat and add enough hot chicken
broth to cover the rice, stir repeatedly, and keep
adding hot broth and stirring until the rice is just
tender. Gently fold in the warm cream and radicchio
and simmer gently until rice is completely tender.

Taste and re-season. Fold in the Parmesan cheese. Serve immediately.

Gamberi alla Piazza San Giovanni Batista

These giant shrimp (or prawns, as they are called in the UK) arrive each week in Lubriano from the Adriatic Coast. They arrive with heads on and are sugar-sweet and bright orange in color. The fish truck owner told me to cook them this way!

2 servings

12 giant shrimp or prawns, heads and shells on
¼ cup butter
¼ cup olive oil
3 cloves garlic, whole
Salt
Tabasco
Lemon juice

Heat a very heavy skillet to a high heat and add the butter, olive oil, and garlic. Season the shrimp with salt and Tabasco and then immediately add the shrimp to the pan. Take a heavy spatula and press the shrimp down into the pan as hard as you can so that the shrimp shells become a deep, crusty brown. Turn over and repeat. Drizzle with a little lemon juice and serve immediately.

Notes

Bolsena's Sauteed *Corregone*

On the shores of Lake Bolsena, just a ten-minute drive from Lubriano, you can enjoy a moist and succulent fish called corregone. *This is a type of trout that lives in the ancient lake. In fact Dante dined here on his favored dish, the famous Lake Bolsena eels. Numerous lakeside restaurants serve these eels, and the* corregone *too, with French fries, lemon juice, and a side salad. The flesh of the fish is a little meatier than trout, and anglers say the fish puts up quite a fight for its size.*

2 servings

2 *corregone* or trout, butterflied
Salt and pepper
1 sprig freshly picked rosemary, finely chopped
¼ cup olive oil
¼ cup butter
Lemon juice

Heat the oven to broil. Heat a large, heavy skillet and add the olive oil, butter, and rosemary. Place the seasoned fish skin side up into the hot oil with the rosemary and cook until a warm brown color. Turn the fish over, drizzle with a little lemon juice, and place the fish under the broiler to crisp it up a little, being careful not to overcook. Serve with Rosemary Roasted Potatoes (*recipe page 343).

Notes

Signora Gaspari's $6,000 Rabbit

When Signora Gaspari brought me the peace offering of a rabbit, she insisted I cook it this way. In Lubriano, they don't deviate from recipes passed down from generation to generation. Serve it with a plain lettuce salad.

4 servings

1 rabbit (or chicken), cleaned and quartered
Salt and pepper
¼ cup olive oil
2 cloves garlic
2 fresh sprigs rosemary
2 fresh sprigs sage
1 onion, chopped
2 carrots, chopped
1 cup white wine
10 olives, pitted

Season the rabbit with salt and pepper. Heat a heavy skillet and brown the rabbit in the olive oil on top of the stove. Place the rabbit in a heavy roasting pan.

Turn the oven to 325°F. Place the garlic, rosemary, sage, onion, and carrots around the rabbit and pour on the wine. Sprinkle the olives in. Cook uncovered for 2 hours, turning rabbit occasionally. Remove the rabbit and make a sauce by pouring a little water or chicken broth into the pan to deglaze, scraping the bottom to remove all the richness from the pan.

Lubriano Chicken *Buione*

This is a fabulous way to cook chicken! It is cooked to a lush brown, but remains moist.

6 servings

1 chicken, deboned skin on and cut into about 8 pieces
3 tablespoons olive oil
3 tablespoons butter
1 sprig rosemary
3 cloves garlic, crushed
1 cup good white wine
Salt and pepper

Season the chicken with salt and pepper. In a very heavy skillet, sauté the chicken in the olive oil and butter with the rosemary and garlic until the chicken is very well browned on all sides. Remove from the stove. Add the wine and return to the stove. Let the pan simmer very, very slowly with the lid off for about 30 minutes until all the wine has evaporated down to just a couple of tablespoons. If desired, spoon the remaining juices over the chicken before serving.

ॐ

Notes

Herbed Chicken with Lemon and Garlic

Here is a simple way to cook chicken in a hurry!

4 servings

1 whole small chicken, quartered, preferably with skin
   on
½ cup olive oil
3 tablespoon dried mixed herbs or Diana's Fresh Herb
   Mixture (*recipe page 285)
4 cloves garlic
4 slices lemon
Salt and pepper

Heat a large, flat, ovenproof pan on top of the stove until sizzling. Coat the chicken in the oil, salt, and pepper and rub in the dried herbs. Place the chicken skin side down in the pan and leave for a few minutes until almost charred. Turn over and turn down the heat. Place the 4 cloves of garlic and the 4 lemon slices in the pan and place each quarter of chicken on top. Cover the pan well and simmer gently on low for 20 minutes or until chicken is cooked.

❧❧

Notes

❧❧

Hearth-Roasted Quail Stuffed with Rosemary and Garlic

This dish is cooked in the fireplace. If you prefer, use a barbecue.

6 servings

6 quail
Good Umbrian olive oil
Salt
6 cloves garlic
6 short sprigs fresh rosemary

Rub a chestnut roaster with olive oil and set in the fire to heat while preparing the quail. Wipe the quail inside and out. Rub the quail with olive oil. Sprinkle salt into each cavity and add the whole garlic clove and the rosemary. Place the quail in the well-heated chestnut roaster towards the edge of the fire. The quail will take about 30 minutes to cook. Turn occasionally for even cooking. The quail should be slightly charred to give a pleasing smoky flavor.

Notes

Luigina's Goose with Caramelized Onions

8 servings

One 12-pound goose
10 white onions, peeled
6 carrots, halved
¼ cup olive oil
1 cup dry white wine
Salt and pepper

Heat the oven to 450°F. Discard any loose fat from the goose. Remove the neck. Rinse the goose inside and out and pat dry. Season the cavity of the goose very well with salt and pepper. Place the goose in a heavy roasting pan with the whole onions and carrots. Pour the olive oil and wine over the goose and place in the oven. Cook at 450°F for 30 minutes, then turn the heat down to 325°F. Roast slowly, basting frequently for 3 hours or until the juices run clear when a thigh is pierced. Remove the goose to a platter and surround with the onions and carrots. Remove the fat from the top of any remaining gravy and serve alongside the goose.

ॐ◈

Notes

ॐ◈

Grilled Sausage with Rosemary, Onion, and Garlic

If you leave out the garlic, this is a good dish for breakfast, too.

4 servings

1 pound Italian sausage links
Good olive oil
2 onions chopped
2 cloves garlic chopped
4 large sprigs fresh rosemary

Heat a stove-top solid grill for at least 10 minutes. Brush the surface with olive oil. Place the sausages on the grill, spreading them out with space in between. Sprinkle the onion and garlic in between the sausages. Now lay the rosemary between the sausages. Don't be afraid to get the sausage and rosemary a good crusty brown.

❧❧

Notes

❧❧

Maiale in Casseruola –
Roast Pork Casserole with Orvieto Classico
Wine, Fennel, and Red Peppers

6 servings

One 4-pound pork roast
½ cup pancetta or bacon
¼ cup olive oil
1 bulb fennel, chopped
2 onions, chopped
2 cloves garlic, crushed
1 red bell pepper, chopped
½ teaspoon fennel seeds
Salt and generous red pepper
2 cups good Orvieto Classico white wine

Heat a heavy casserole. Brown the pancetta in olive oil and add the fennel, onion, garlic, bell pepper, and fennel seeds. Add the pork roast. Season to taste. Add the wine and simmer, covered, in the oven for at least 3 hours at 325°F.

Notes

Giuseppina's Spit-Roasted *Porchetta* with Fennel and Sage

In Italy, the skin is left on the pork to produce a delicious crackling—not so in the USA! Porchetta is often served at road side stands. It's scrumptious served on panini.

12 servings

One pork loin boneless roast, approximately 6 pounds
4 ounces pig's liver (optional)
4 cloves garlic, chopped
1 onion, chopped
½ cup olive oil
½ cup white wine
1 cup chopped fennel fronds
2 cups chopped sage
Salt
Pepper
Ground *peperoncino*

Place the loin of pork, fat side down, on a large cutting board. Cut the loin longitudinally about 2 inches deep, to make a long cavity for the stuffing. Sauté the garlic and onion in the olive oil. Add the liver and sauté until brown. Add the wine and simmer until the wine has evaporated. Add the fennel, sage, salt, and pepper and place this stuffing in the slit cavity of the loin. Roll and tie together tightly with string, fat side out. Rub the fat liberally with salt, pepper, and *peperoncino*. Roast slowly on a spit for at least four hours until a crusty brown. Set aside for at least one hour before carving. Serve hot or cold.

Giuseppina's Loin of Pork Roast with Sage

This is an excellent dish to serve on Christmas Eve—it is succulent and has warm, friendly flavors.

12 servings

One 6-pound whole loin of pork, bone-in and chined
Salt and pepper
4 large sprigs of sage
6 Italian sausages, skinned
6 chopped scallions
1 cup chopped celery
10 olives
1 cup good olive oil
3 cups white Orvieto Classico wine

Heat the oven to 500°F. Chine the pork by slicing the meat from the bone, but don't cut it all the way through, so that the meat creates a "flap" that can be returned to the bone. Rub the skin side of the meat very well with salt and pepper and rub well with olive oil. Place the sage and then the sausage meat and scallions into the cavity and fold the flap of meat back onto the bone, securing it in place with a couple of skewers. Place in a large roasting pan surrounding the roast with the celery and olives. Pour in the wine and then the olive oil. Place in the oven for 20 minutes at 500°F and then turn the heat down to 325°F for at least 3 hours, spooning the juices over the meat every

30 minutes. Cook until all the juices have evaporated and the roast becomes brown and crispy. Set aside to rest the meat for about 15 minutes before carving.

Bistecca Fiorentina – Florentine Steak

In Italy, Chiana beef is used for this famous Florentine steak, which is extremely flavorful but not as tender as American beef. It is usually cooked over an open fire, but a barbecue works just fine too!

6 servings

One 3-pound Porterhouse steak, on the bone, about 2
    or 3 inches thick
Salt, freshly cracked pepper
4 sprigs of rosemary

Heat the barbecue to an extremely high heat. Rub the steak with lots of salt and pepper and tie with sprigs of rosemary on either side of the steak. Place the steak on the hot, hot barbecue until the rosemary chars away. This steak is usually served rare in the middle. Cook on each side, depending on the thickness, about 10 minutes. Take the steak off the coals and set aside for 15 minutes. Cut the meat from the bone and carve thinly vertically.

Notes

Slow-Roasted Veal Cooked in Wine with a Topping of Crispy Mushrooms

10 servings

One 3-pound veal or pork roast
½ cup olive oil, divided in half
½ cup butter, divided in half
4 cloves garlic, peeled
Salt and pepper
1 cup Orvieto Classico or dry white wine
1 pound assorted mushrooms, cut into grape-size
    pieces
1 cup vegetable bouillon

Heat a heavy casserole on medium-high heat. Brown the veal in half the olive oil and half the butter with the garlic. Season to taste. Pour the wine into the casserole, cover and place in a 325°F oven for three hours to simmer gently. About an hour before serving, heat the remaining olive oil and butter in a heavy saucepan. Add the mushrooms, salt, and pepper and cook over high heat until lightly brown. Add the bouillon and simmer, uncovered, until the broth has evaporated and the mushrooms get crispy. Spoon over the roast just before serving.

❦❦

Notes

❦❦

Scallopine di Vitello alla Griglia – Grilled Veal Cutlets

4 servings

1 pound veal cutlets
¼ cup good olive oil
1½ cups fresh breadcrumbs, mixed with a little fresh
    thyme
Salt and paprika to taste
Lemon slices

Leave the veal cutlets soaking in the olive oil for about 5 minutes. Mix the salt and paprika in with the breadcrumbs and press onto both sides of the veal cutlets. Rub a ridged solid stove-top grill with olive oil and place on medium-high heat for 5 minutes. Add the cutlets and cook until the crumbs are very brown. Serve right away with lemon.

Notes

Spicy Roasted Bagnoregio Vegetables

8 servings

1 head of fennel
1 red bell pepper
1 green bell pepper
3 zucchini
1 medium eggplant
1 leek or onion
¼ cup olive oil
½ teaspoon hot chili powder
2 tablespoons Diana's Fresh Herb Mix (*recipe page
    285)
Salt and pepper

Heat the oven to 450°F. Slice all the vegetables in large ½-inch slices. Sprinkle the eggplant with a little salt and set aside for 15 minutes. Rinse the eggplant and pat dry. Toss all the vegetables in a mix of the olive oil, chili powder, and Diana's Fresh Herb Mixture. Season to taste. Place in the oven and cook the vegetables for about 30 minutes or until a warm toasty brown.

Notes

Rosemary Roasted Potatoes

This recipe belongs to my long-time cooking partner Wendy. She just took a Tuscan potato recipe and made it better by smashing the potatoes down with a glass before placing them in the oven!

4 servings

2 pounds new potatoes, boiled for 8 minutes
1 sprig fresh rosemary, leaves removed from stalk
½ cup good olive oil
Salt and lots of pepper

Heat the oven to broil for at least 5 minutes. Pat the boiled potatoes dry. Grease a cookie sheet. Smash each potato down onto a cookie sheet with the bottom of a glass. Drizzle the potatoes with the olive oil, sprinkle with rosemary and salt and lots of pepper, and place under the broiler at least 6 inches away from the heat source for 5 to 10 minutes or until deep brown and cooked.

Notes

Slow-Roasted Onions with Breadcrumbs

Here is another of Pierro's delectable dishes. He cooks his onions in his cooling-down pizza oven. You can make this dish at home, too, in a regular oven.

6 servings

2 pounds small white onions, peeled
½ cup water
½ cup olive oil
Salt and white pepper
2 cups breadcrumbs made with stale bread

Place all the onions in a baking dish, packing them together so that they are almost touching. Pour the water and olive oil over the onions and season liberally with salt and white pepper. Now sprinkle the breadcrumbs onto the dish and place in the oven at 250°F, uncovered, for 3 to 4 hours or until a warm, toasty brown.

Notes

Anthony's Grilled Fresh Figs

This is not truly a Lubriano recipe; my son Anthony requested I make it for him. A chef had served it to him in some fancy New York Hotel! We've used the idea (for it is hardly a recipe) time and time again as a last-minute after-dinner treat. We pick fresh figs off the tree in our garden and place them directly under the broiler. When figs are ripe and plentiful I freeze some for use in cooking this recipe during the winter.

4 servings

12 large fresh figs (cut in half longitudinally)
¼ cup sugar
8 large scoops *gelato di crema* or vanilla ice cream

Heat the oven to broil for at least 5 minutes. Place the cut figs in four ovenproof ramekins or soup bowls. Sprinkle with sugar and place 6 inches from the heat source. Watch carefully, as they burn easily! Remove when crispy brown, and serve immediately with vanilla ice cream or *gelato*.

≈≈

Notes

Gelato di Crema
If you don't have an ice cream machine, you can still make this recipe!

6 servings

¾ cup sugar
4 egg yolks
1 cup whole milk (microwave 15 seconds)
A pinch of salt
1 finger-length slice of lemon peel (yellow only, no
    white)
1 cup heavy cream

Place a double boiler on top of the stove. Place a cup of water in the bottom. In the meanwhile, beat together the sugar and egg yolks until a very pale yellow and thick. Very slowly add the room-temperature milk, beating very gently with a whisk. Add the lemon peel and salt and place the mixture in the top of the double boiler. Now bring the water below to a very low, gentle boil and stir constantly for about 8 to 10 minutes, until the mixture begins to thicken enough to coat the back of a wooden spoon. Cover and place in the refrigerator until completely cold.

Whip cream. Remove the lemon peel from mixture and fold in the whipped cream. Transfer to an ice cream machine, or place in your freezer and gently fold the mixture with a wooden spoon every 30 minutes until set.

❧❧

Notes

Tiramisu

The name of this coffee-flavored treat means "pick me up" in Italian.

Unfortunately, in the USA everyone is very nervous about cooking with uncooked egg yolks. My friends in Italy say that the salmonella comes from the outside of the egg and not the inside. There, they take the time to really wash and dry their eggs before making this dish. It all depends on how desperate you are for the taste. Be it on your own head! Any dietitian in the USA would tell you not to serve raw eggs.

8 servings

Dipping liquid:
2 cups very strong coffee
2 tablespoons sugar
10 ounces lady fingers

Mousse:
4 eggs separated
¾ cup sugar
½ cup Cognac
1 pound mascarpone

Topping:
1½ cups cream
Cocoa powder

Whisk the egg yolks with a little sugar until they are really white and fluffy, gradually add the rest of the sugar, and then add the cognac. Add the mascarpone and gently folding in. Beat the egg whites until stiff and gradually add, very carefully, folding into the yolk mixture.

Dip the lady fingers into the dipping mixture and layer with the egg mixture, finishing with a layer of egg mixture. Spread with whipped cream. Just before serving, sprinkle with cocoa powder. Preferably let sit overnight.

Cecily's Pavlova with Mixed Wild Berries and Cream

6 servings

4 egg whites
2 cups white sugar
1 teaspoon vanilla extract
1 teaspoon cornstarch
3 cups wild mixed berries tossed in a little *grappa* or
     limoncello
1 cup heavy cream, whipped

Place the egg whites in a bowl and bring them to room temperature. In the meanwhile, mark a 12-inch circle on a sheet of wax paper and set on a cookie sheet. Heat the oven to 300°F. Begin beating the egg whites, then add the sugar very, very gradually. Once the sugar is incorporated, turn up the speed and beat the meringue for 5 minutes until the mixture is a thick, shiny white. Add the vanilla extract and the cornstarch and beat for 1 more minute. Spoon the meringue onto the circle and bake in the oven for 1 hour. Don't remove the Pavlova from the oven; just switch off the oven and leave inside for one hour. Store in an airtight container until ready for use. Just before serving, spoon the berries on top and then top with cream.

Notes

Panna Cotta with Fresh Figs

4 to 6 servings

3 cups heavy cream
1 cup milk
2 cups confectioners' sugar
1 vanilla bean, split open lengthwise
1 tablespoon gelatin, softened in 2 tablespoons boiling
    water
10 figs, each sliced open to look like a flower

In a heavy pan, mix together the cream, milk, and sugar. Add the vanilla bean and gently bring to a boil. Reduce to low and simmer gently for 7 minutes. Remove from the stove and add the softened gelatin, stirring to make sure the gelatin is incorporated. Pour the mixture into individual greased ramekins or into a low, flat mold. Chill for 4 hours or longer. Turn out onto a platter and decorate with figs and rose petals.

❧❧

Notes

❧❧

Festa Delle Donne Mimosa Cake with *Limoncello*

This cake is served to celebrate the Festival of the Ladies, which coincides with the very first mimosa flowers appearing after winter. Cake crumbs are sprinkled on top of the cake to resemble the soft yellow blossoms that herald the very beginning of spring.

8 servings

Cake:
1 lemon cake mix (made to package instructions, but substitute half limoncello* and half orange juice instead of water)

Syrup:
¾ cup sugar
¼ cup limoncello
2 tablespoons butter

Frosting:
2 cups confectioners' sugar
¼ cup butter, melted
1 teaspoon finely grated lemon rind
2 to 3 tablespoons lemon juice
1 cup reserved cake crumbs

Prepare the cake mix per package instructions,

substituting *limoncello* and orange juice instead of water. Put the cake mixture into a bundt pan, reserving ½ cup of cake mixture. Bake per package instructions. Cook the ½ cup of reserved mixture separately in a ramekin (this cake is used later for decoration). After 20 minutes the ramekin cake should be ready. Remove, cool well, and crumble into fine pieces. In the meanwhile, make the syrup by bringing to a boil all the syrup ingredients. When the bundt cake is cooked, remove from the pan and slowly pour the syrup on the cake. Set aside for at least 30 minutes to cool.

To make the topping: sift the sugar, then mix together with butter and lemon rind and as much lemon juice as needed to make the frosting spreadable. When the cake is cooled, frost with lemon frosting and sprinkle the reserved cake crumbs over the frosting. Decorate the platter with yellow flowers.

*Limoncello is a liqueur from the Amalfi Coast that can be found in liquor stores throughout the USA.

Recipe Index

Recipes

Acknowledgments

My grateful thanks go to all those who helped me in so many ways to get my book from rusty draft to smart print. My ever-loving thanks go to my husband David for his support and eagle eye in all phases of this book.

For more information, please visit

www.dianagarmstrong.com

22267158R00230

Made in the USA
San Bernardino, CA
27 June 2015